The Recovery Handbook
Understanding Addictions and Evidenced-Based Treatment Practices

Nicholas D. Young, PhD, EdD

Melissa A. Mumby, EdD

Jennifer A. Smolinski, JD

Series in Sociology

VERNON PRESS

www.vernonpress.com

In the Americas:	*In the rest of the world:*
Vernon Press	Vernon Press
1000 N West Street,	C/Sancti Espiritu 17,
Suite 1200, Wilmington,	Malaga, 29006
Delaware 19801	Spain
United States	

Series in Sociology

Library of Congress Control Number: 2020935718

ISBN: 978-1-64889-065-9

Also available: 978-1-62273-967-7 [Hardback]; 978-1-64889-014-7 [PDF, E-Book]

Cover design by Vernon Press using elements designed by Freepik.

Table of Contents

Part Three: Resources

Acknowledgement

There is a special class of people who make those around them undoubtedly better. They may not always be the one on center stage, or even care to be, but behind the scenes we all know that their contributions have great meaning. One such person is Mrs. Suzanne "Sue" Clark, who recently retired from a lengthy and highly successful career in the Holyoke and South Hadley Public Schools. As her first official retirement act, she graciously volunteered to edit this book. There is no question that Sue is a seasoned editor and gifted grammarian whose attention to detail made this tome far stronger and much more reader-friendly. This in and of itself would more than warrant this public note of appreciation; however, she has also spent a lifetime modeling kindness to those around her—friends, family, colleagues, and this writing team—so that we may all understand on an even deeper level the importance of positive human connection when navigating the trials and tribulations of everyday life. For this, she has our even deeper respect and gratitude.

Acknowledgment

Foreword

The Recovery Handbook: Understanding Addiction and Evidence-Based Treatment Practices has found its way into your hands for a reason. Before you can begin to figure out why and how you are willing to help people recover from addictions, I would like to share a story. I remember the impact this brief event had on my life as I struggled to put the pieces together in order to assist those suffering towards the health of recovery.

In 2015, I attended a community workshop for parents and teachers designed to raise awareness of the crisis regarding teenage drug and alcohol abuse. A young man, about twenty-five years old, was the guest speaker. He had attended the local elementary school where he began using drugs at the tender age of ten. At 21, and after ten years of drug use, he found himself in a treatment program that helped him find sobriety and saved his life. He was now dedicating his work to creating programs for addicts and youth all over the country. His mission was to share his story of hope.

The guidance counselor from his elementary school was in the audience and asked him what they might have done differently when he was in fifth grade. She wanted to know what might have influenced his decisions at such a young age; after all, there had been a school, a community, his family, his spiritual connection and all the professionals in the town. After a pause, the young man spoke about never understanding what 'self-love' really meant.

> When I was young, no one ever **taught** me about how important I am and that loving myself was more than just an arrogant ego trip. Loving myself meant that I would and could take care of myself, because I developed unconditional love for who I am right now. Regardless of my addictions, my flaws, my history, my mistakes, even my self-hatred and negative criticism of who I was. I had to learn to become my own best friend and hang out with all the parts of me in order to find my way home. And home meant loving myself and my sobriety enough to make the daily, sometimes hourly healthy choices that would catapult me to a thriving and flourishing life.

Addiction knows no limits, boundaries, class, social or economic parameters, no gender, no age or race. Addiction is a chronic disease compromising brain function - it takes lives, destroys dreams, ravages families, fills our jails, terrifies our youth, costs our economy trillions and continues to fray the fabric of our society.

If we turn our focus and look in the rearview mirror of the addiction epidemic, we can find our focus on recovery. In fact, the addiction crisis has brought this country to a point where almost everyone knows someone who is in recovery. Addiction has no cure; rather, there are solutions to healing.

The 2014 movie *The Anonymous People,* directed by Greg Williams, is just one invaluable resource to building a tool-kit of skills, knowledge and sensitivity to the struggle of finding ways to help those who suffer from addictions.

According to the Substance Abuse and Mental Health Services Administration, (2019) and the National Institute on Drug Abuse (2018h), the statistics on drug abuse are extremely sobering and include:

- 164.8 million people, aged 12 and older, have used addictive substances,

- 25 million suffer from the disease of addiction,

- 2/3 of all American families are touched by addiction,

- 740 billion dollars annually - the cost to our economy for untreated addiction in the workplace, healthcare expenses and crimes in the community,

- 20 million individuals are suffering in silence,

- An estimated 65% of those incarcerated have a connection to addiction.

The good news is that the 'rearview mirror' glance has over 23 million people living in long-term recovery. Sobriety is the silent antidote and remedy – it is a hopeful alternative to addiction. There is an army of silent voices eager and willing to support others suffering from a disease that requires so much more than 'just say no.' It is time to use all the resources available to find ways to stay with the addict, regardless of the drug of choice. To help them find solutions, treatment programs, clinics, support networks, alternatives and even beds in times of crisis.

The terrain of dealing with addictions is unpredictable, tumultuous, and constantly changing. The courage to embark on this journey is filled with others who have gone before you. Look to the experts, the guides, and stand on the shoulders of those who know the territory. Stay connected with supervision, colleagues, the latest research and anything new that might support the healing afforded those who suffer.

Congratulations on your willingness to embark upon this most delicate of the helping professions. You have picked up this book because there is something drawing you to enter prepared into this field of healing. You can use this book as a 'pocket guide' to help you navigate the various hills and valleys on the road to helping someone manage their addiction and find ways to live a productive, and positive life. You will find your own way to understand what recovery really looks like for each and every individual suffering with their personal and unique addictions.

Keep in mind as you build your skills and knowledge in this field that you could be the only caring guide in an addict's life. You might want to think of them as struggling with a diagnosis of cancer, heart disease, diabetes, or some medical disease, as an addiction of any kind is no different. By reframing the disease, it provides a doorway into compassion and hope which is often closed to addicts. The addict often finds a dead end in treatment when relapsing, leaving the program or overdosing - rest assured, the addict will relapse, it is part of the healing.

Just as we would continue to find treatments for cancer patients, it is paramount that we continue to find treatments that work for those suffering from addictions. Unconditional love, acceptance, positive regard, hope and compassionate responses must become the threads that hold the treatment programs together long enough to ensure sobriety. We are talking about stepping up the love, compassion and care we have for each other and our efforts to win the ongoing and relentless fight in this war that is taking so many lives.

Often relapse sends us and the medical community into blaming the patient for not sticking to the program and pulling out the support. Addiction has no cure, but it does have a solution. Find ways to open the hearts of all those who have suffered from the debilitating disease of addiction and are on the road to recovery. Remember my young friend who had to be taught about self-love. Develop a practice of loving yourself first in order to teach others how to do the same. Take care of yourself while you learn to care for others. Trust that you are in this field for a reason and all those you touch with your wisdom, light and hope are already grateful.

Gena M. Rotas, LICSW, author

Love YOU! Small Changes to Quiet the Gremlins and Tame those Unhealthy Habits, Behaviors and Addictions

Part One:
Substance Addictions

Chapter 1

Introduction to Addictions and Evidenced-Based Practices: Statistics and the Devastating Nature of Addiction

Addictions are not limited to drugs and alcohol. There are also addictions to gambling, food, sex/hypersexuality, shopping, and virtual reality. Each type of addiction carries with it compulsive behaviors that the user may not even realize. This intense focus towards a particular item or category may be so strong that it monopolizes the individual's entire life and strangles out all family, friends, work or enjoyable events. To set the record straight, an addiction is "a complex condition, a brain disease that is manifested by compulsive ... [behaviors] ... despite harmful consequences" (American Psychiatric Association, 2017).

Drug Addictions

Individuals begin using drugs for a myriad of reasons. While some people may begin using drugs to impress their friends, fit in, rebel parental authority, or improve their cognitive and/or athletic performance, others use drugs for the intense feelings of pleasure, power, self-confidence, satisfaction, increased energy and/or relaxation that they provide (American Psychiatric Association, 2017). Other individuals begin using drugs in order to feel better or self-medicate. Those who suffer from social anxiety, stress-related disorders, and depression will abuse drugs in an attempt to lessen their feelings of distress (American Psychiatric Association, 2017; National Institute on Drug Abuse, 2018a).

The use and abuse of and addiction to illicit drugs, prescription drugs, alcohol, and nicotine has a direct effect on crime, health care costs and productivity and cost Americans more than $740 billion in 2016 alone (U.S. Department of Health and Human Services, 2018). Drug and alcohol abuse and addiction has also contributed to the death of more than 150,000 Americans (U.S. Department of Health and Human Services, 2018). During the 20th century alone, approximately 100 million individuals died from tobacco addiction worldwide, and if smoking trends continue along the same path, the projected cumulative death toll for the 21st century is set to reach 1 billion (Jha et al., 2006).

Drug abuse and addiction and its harmful consequences are gender and age-neutral and affect all individuals. Babies who are exposed to drugs while in their mother's womb may be born premature and underweight and have a slower track of intellectual and behavioral development than those babies who were not exposed (Ross, Graham, Money & Stanwood, 2015). Adolescent drug abusers are more likely to act out, have poor academic performance, drop out of school, have unplanned pregnancies, and are more at risk for violence and infectious diseases than their non-abusive peers (Lander, Howsare & Byrne, 2013).

Adult drug abusers will most likely suffer from trouble thinking clearly, remembering, and paying attention in addition to poor social behavior, work performance and personal relationships (Lander et al., 2013). Children of drug-addicted parents are often subjected to chaotic, stress-filled homes, child abuse and neglect, and are primed and ready for future drug abuse, as evidenced by a national drug use survey that indicates children are using drugs as early as ages 12-13 (U.S. Department of Health and Human Services, 2018).

In addition to the many individual harmful consequences that come with addiction, drug abuse can cause serious health problems for others. An expectant mother's use of heroin, for example, can cause neonatal abstinence syndrome (withdrawal) in the baby once it is born. Children who have been exposed to drugs may need educational support in the classroom to address deficits in developmental areas such as behavior, attention, and thinking (Solis, Shadur, Burns & Hussong, 2012). According to the Surgeon General (Naeem, 2015), those individuals who have been involuntarily exposed to environmental tobacco smoke (secondhand smoke) are at a 20-30% increased risk for heart disease and lung cancer.

The abuse of all drugs, particularly those that are injected, is a major contributing factor to the spread of infectious diseases (Schwetz, Calder, Rosenthal, Kattakuzhy & Fauci, 2019). Injectable drugs such as heroin, cocaine, and methamphetamine account for approximately 12% of new AIDS cases and perpetuate the spread of hepatitis B and C as well as other sexually transmitted diseases (Schwetz et al., 2019).

Opioid Crisis

Starting in the late 1990s, healthcare providers began to prescribe opioid pain relievers after assurances from pharmaceutical companies that patients would not become addicted to the drugs (National Institute on Drug Abuse, 2019b). As a result, opioid overdose rates increased and in 2017, "more than 47,000 Americans died as a result of an opioid overdose, including prescription opioids, heroin, and illicitly manufactured fentanyl" (National Institute on Drug Abuse, 2019b, n.p.). Perhaps more compelling was that more than 652,000 individuals were afflicted by heroin use disorder and approximately three times that number suffered from opioid substance abuse disorders (National Institute on Drug Abuse, 2019b).

The misuse of and addiction to opioids, including prescription pain relievers, currently causes the death of approximately 130 people per day (Centers for Disease Control and Prevention, 2018c; 2019a). This national crisis not only affects public health, but the social and economic welfare of the nation as evidenced by the estimate of "$78.5 billion a year, including the costs of health care, lost productivity, addiction treatment, and criminal justice involvement" (Florence, Zhou, Luo & Xu, 2016, p. 901).

While prescription opioids can be used to treat moderate-to-severe pain and are often prescribed following surgery or injury, there has been a dramatic increase in the acceptance and use of prescription opioids for the treatment of chronic, non-cancer pain despite the known serious risks and the lack of evidence related to long-term effectiveness (Centers for Disease Control and Prevention, 2018c). In 2017, more than 191 million opioid prescriptions were dispensed, with a wide variation across the United States. Research shows that health care providers in Alabama wrote the most prescriptions, 3 times as many as the lowest prescribing state of Hawaii, and this regional variation cannot be accounted for by the underlying health status of the states' populations (Centers for Disease Control and Prevention, 2017).

Evidence shows that more than 30% of overdoses involving opioids also involve benzodiazepines (Centers for Disease Control and Prevention, 2018c). Between 1996 and 2013, benzodiazepine prescriptions increased from 8.1 million to 13.5 million, a 67% increase (Lembke, 2018; National Institute on Drug Abuse, 2018e). The main cause of an overdose fatality includes combining opioids and benzodiazepines as "both types of drug sedate users and suppress breathing" (National Institute on Drug Abuse, 2018e). Research studies highlight this danger as they have found that the overdose death rate among individuals receiving both types of medications was 10 times higher than among those only receiving opioids (National Institute on Drug Abuse, 2018e).

Heroin

Recently, the use of heroin has greatly increased in demographic groups with historically low rates of use, such as women, the privately insured, and people with higher incomes (Center for Disease Control and Prevention, 2019c). In

2017, approximately 494,000 people age 12 and older reported using heroin in America alone, and in "2015, 81,326 emergency department visits occurred for unintentional, heroin-related poisonings ... an estimated rate of almost 26 per 100,000 people" (Center for Disease Control and Prevention, 2019c). During 2017 in the United States, more than 15,000 people died from drug overdoses involving heroin with males aged 25-44 having the highest heroin death rate at 14.8 per 100,000 (Center for Disease Control and Prevention, 2019c).

Cocaine

In the United States alone, approximately 2% or 5 million Americans were involved in the use of cocaine in 2016 (Centers for Disease Control and Prevention, 2019a). Evidence shows that cocaine was involved in 1 in 5 overdose deaths, approximately 14,000 people, during 2017 (Centers for Disease Control and Prevention, 2019a). Perhaps surprisingly, the highest rate of death occurred among non-Hispanic blacks in the Washington, D.C. and Ohio areas (Centers for Disease Control and Prevention, 2019a).

Psychostimulants

There are two types of psychostimulants – prescription drugs such as those used to treat depression and attention-deficit hyperactivity disorder (ADHD) and illicit drugs such as ecstasy and methamphetamine (Center for Disease Control and Prevention, 2019a). In 2016, those who misused this drug class included an estimated 6 million Americans age 12 and older, which led to a 2017 death rate of more than 10,000 people, a 37% increase from the prior year (Center for Disease Control and Prevention, 2019a). Evidence shows that overdoses occurred more often in the non-Hispanic white ethnic group, although the "largest absolute rate change in psychostimulant-involved overdoses was in the American Indian/Alaska Native populations" (Center for Disease Control and Prevention, 2019a, n.p.).

Marijuana

Marijuana contains mind-altering psychoactive compounds like tetrahydrocannabinol, or THC, as well as other active compounds like cannabidiol, or CBD, that are not mind-altering, and its effects on an individual depend on the individual's previous experience with drugs, genetics, gender, route of administration, and potency (National Institute on Drug Abuse, 2019e). In 2017, an estimated 26 million Americans aged 12 and older used marijuana. Of these individuals, 4 million were classified as having a marijuana use disorder as the recurrent use of the drug caused clinically significant impairment, including health problems and failure to meet major responsibilities at work, school, or home (Bose, Hedden, Lipari, & Park-Lee, 2018; National Center on Drug Abuse, 2019e).

Polysubstances

Polysubstance drug use occurs when more than one drug is used simultaneously, which can substantially increase the chances for drug overdose (Centers for Disease Control and Prevention, 2019d). Those with a polysubstance abuse issue tend to prefer the high associated with the use of multiple drugs, rather than the particular drug (Centers for Disease Control and Prevention, 2019d). Common combinations of drugs can include "illicitly-manufactured fentanyl (IMF) and heroin; illicitly-manufactured fentanyl and cocaine; heroin and methamphetamine; and prescription or illicit opioids and benzodiazepines" (Centers for Disease Control and Prevention, 2019d, n.p.).

Synthetic opioids, in combination with other drugs, such as prescription opioids, heroin, and alcohol, accounted for 80% of deaths related to drug overdose (Centers for Disease Control and Prevention, 2019d). Cocaine accounts for 72.2% of polysubstance overdose deaths and this trend is increasing (Centers for Disease Control and Prevention, 2019d).

Fentanyl

Fentanyl contamination of illegal drugs has led to an increase in drug-related deaths as it is 50 times stronger than heroin and is often, and unknowingly to the drug user, "mixed into counterfeit opioid pills, heroin, cocaine, and methamphetamine" (Centers for Disease Control and Prevention, 2019d, n.p.). Fentanyl was responsible for approximately 57% of the deaths due to overdose in which cocaine, heroin, or methamphetamine was also a factor, according to a ten-state study and this number is increasing daily (Center for Disease Control and Prevention, 2019d).

The Relationship Between Drugs and the Human Brain

The most intricate organ in the body is the brain (National Institute on Drug Abuse, 2014a). It consists of many parts that work together and are "responsible for coordinating and performing specific functions" (National Institute on Drug Abuse, 2014a, p. 17). The brain stem, cerebral cortex and the limbic system act as a three-way agent responsible for all basic bodily functions, responses to experiences, and shaping behaviors, emotions and thoughts (National Institute on Drug Abuse, 2014a). The brain is the center of communication and consists of "billions of neurons, or nerve cells, that pass messages back and forth among the different structures housed within the brain, the spinal cord, and the nerves contained in the rest of the body" (National Institute on Drug Abuse, 2014a, p. 16).

Drugs affect the brain by tapping into its communication system and interfering with the way neurons normally send, receive, and process information (National Institute on Drug Abuse, 2014a). Although drugs can mimic the brain's own natural chemicals, they do not activate neurons in the same way. The chemical structure of heroin and marijuana mimics natural neurotransmitters and fools the receptors into activating and attaching to neurons (National Institute on Drug Abuse, 2014a). The messages the neurons receive are atypical and cause the brain to become confused and eventually shut down (National Institute on Drug Abuse, 2014a).

Most drugs produce high levels of dopamine, which is then sent to the reward center in the brain, creating a sense of euphoria. This 'high' is reinforced repeatedly by the drug and eventually the brain requires more dopamine in order to receive the same feelings of excitement and overstimulation (U.S. Department of Health and Human Services, 2018). Research has shown that some drugs can immediately release 2 to 10 times the amount of dopamine that the natural rewards from eating and sex do, leading to long-lasting effects that overwhelm the pleasure circuits of the brain (Harvard Health Publishing, 2011). As drug use continues, the "brain adapts by reducing the ability of cells in the reward circuit to respond to it," (National Institute on Drug Abuse, 2018g, n.p.). The feeling of euphoria that was felt the first time the drug was used is therefore reduced and creates a tolerance that then requires more of the preferred drug (National Institute on Drug Abuse, 2018g).

Defining Drug Addiction

Addiction is a "chronic, relapsing disorder characterized by compulsive drug seeking, continued use despite harmful consequences, and long-lasting changes in the brain" (U.S. Department of Health and Human Services, 2018, p. 1). While an individual's initial decision to take drugs may be voluntary and for any number of reasons, the brain changes that occur with such use interfere with an individual's self-control and their ability to resist the intense urges to repetitively use a drug (National Institute on Drug Abuse, 2018g). Individuals who use and misuse drugs have distorted thinking, behavior, and bodily functions, "have an intense focus on using a certain substance … to the point that it takes over their life" (American Psychiatric Association, 2017, n.p.). Despite the knowledge that it is interfering with their normal daily activities and life, they continue to use the drug or drugs of choice (American Psychiatric Association, 2017).

Symptoms of Addiction

The signs and symptoms of drug addiction can fall in 4 categories:
Impaired control: a craving or strong urge to use the substance; desire or failed attempts to cut down or control substance use
Social problems: substance use causes failure to complete major tasks at work, school or home; social, work or leisure activities are given up or cut back due to substance use
Risky use: substance use occurs in risky settings; continued use despite known problems
Drug effects: tolerance … withdrawal symptoms
(American Psychiatric Association, 2017, n.p.).

Susceptibility to Addiction

An individual's decision to take drugs is typically voluntary; however, with continued use, their ability to exert self-control can become seriously impaired. Brain imaging studies have shown that the brain changes due to addiction include behavior control, decision making, judgment, and learning/memory (Fowler et al., 2007; National Institute on Drug Abuse, 2014a).

Akin to other diseases, the vulnerability to addiction differs from one individual to another. The National Institute on Drug Abuse (2018g) has stated that through research it has been found that there is a great likelihood of drug abuse and addiction when there are multiple risk factors, while increased protective factors can substantially reduce the chances of addiction (National Institute on Drug Abuse, 2014a). There are both risk and protective factors for each of six categories to include environmental, biological, family, education, individual, and personality (Alaska Division of Behavioral Health, 2011).

Behavioral Addictions

Addiction is commonly thought of as addiction to alcohol, drugs, and smoking yet evidence shows that 1 in 8 individuals are addicted to behaviors that do not involve the use of a substance (Alavi et al., 2012; Iliades, 2016). Behavioral addictions involve an activity or behavior that provides a means of coping or escaping reality, such as sex, surfing the internet, or participating in adrenaline sports and result in the same changes in mood, increasing levels of tolerance, withdrawal and relapse found with substance abuse (Northpoint Recovery, 2017). Behavioral addictions do not involve drugs or alcohol; however, they may have the same effects long-term as they may "take over a person's life and tear families apart, causing emotional trauma, financial problems and can cause serious physical problems" Northpoint Recovery, 2017, n.p.).

Food

Eating disorders, such as anorexia nervosa, bulimia nervosa, and compulsive eating have become more prevalent due in part to the appeal of unhealthy foods. Advertising in the media and the dominating and growing fast-food culture coupled with unrealistic body image messages on social media and television have caused unattainable goals; thus producing a dysfunction with food that can be traced to food addiction (Northpoint Recovery, 2017).

Gambling

Gambling, such as the lottery, scratch tickets, football pools, bingo, horse racing, and casinos, has increased due to their accessibility and acceptability and is the one behavioral addiction that most closely resembles drug and alcohol addiction (Northpoint Recovery, 2017; Iliades, 2016). Research has shown that gambling addiction illuminates the same area of the brain as drug addiction and that treatment for gambling addiction is included in the same genre of therapy that is used for those addicted to drugs and alcohol (Northpoint Recovery, 2017).

Internet

Internet addiction, such as gaming, cybersex, and shopping, has reached global proportions with addicts spending up to 11 hours a day on the internet, risking their family and peer relationships, employment, and education while feeling unable to stop and experiencing feelings of guilt and withdrawal (Gentile et al., 2011).

Sex

Sex addiction has not been formally classified as an addiction by the American Psychiatric Association, yet the symptoms of sex addiction, such as a total disregard for dangers, risks and consequences mirror those of alcohol and drug addiction (Iliades, 2016). For this reason, those afflicted with a sex addiction seem to respond well to a 12-step treatment program (Iliades, 2016; Psychology Today, n.d.).

Shopping

Research has demonstrated that approximately 6% of the population suffers from compulsive shopping that results in guilt, depression and often financial issues (Heshmat, 2018). More than 80% of all individuals with a shopping addiction are women; however, due to the internet and the ability to purchase online, it is expected that more men may struggle with over-shopping (Heshmat, 2018).

Video games

Video games are highly addictive and have become even more so by allowing players to build or assume an alternative identity and interact with others across the world. Research has shown that video games have affected both children and adults, with 1 in 10 boys considered out of control, causing symptoms that seriously interfere with their work, school, family, and psychological functioning (Gonsalves, 2007).

Work

Although working too much is seen as a positive attribute and is associated with financial status and self-identity, it has the ability to ruin relationships and an individual's health. More than 10,000 people die every year in Japan from working too many hours (Weller, 2017).

Pharmacotherapies

Pharmacotherapies are therapies that employ the use of specific drugs to combat and rehabilitate individuals who have a history of drug abuse (Koob, Lloyd & Mason, 2009). All of the drugs listed below are generally more effective when used in combination with therapy (National Institute on Drug Abuse, 2018h).

Opioid Addiction

Buprenorphine. This synthetic opioid medication is able to reduce or eliminate the effects of withdrawal due to its ability to partially block opioid receptors (National Institute on Drug Abuse, 2018h). In addition to its pure form, buprenorphine can be combined with the drug naloxone. When this combination is taken as prescribed, the naloxone has no effect, yet when an individual addicted to opioids ingests the combination, naloxone "produces severe withdrawal symptoms" (National Institute on Drug Abuse, 2018h, p. 41).

Methadone. Used to block the effects of illicit opioids, reduce cravings and prevent withdrawal symptoms, this drug is a "long acting synthetic opioid agonist medication" (National Institute on Drug Abuse, 2018h, p. 39).

Naltrexone®. This synthetic opioid antagonist can reverse opioid overdose and treat opioid addiction by blocking "opioids from binding to their receptors" (National Institute on Drug Abuse, 2018h, p. 42) and preventing a feeling of euphoria.

Tobacco Addiction

Any of the pharmacotherapies listed below may be combined with behavioral interventions, including group and individual therapies, which will amplify the effects of medication by assisting individuals in stress management, the recognition and avoidance of high-risk situations for smoking relapse, and the development of alternative coping strategies (National Institute on Drug Abuse, 2018h).

Bupropion. More commonly known as the anti-depressant Wellbutrin®, this drug produces a mild stimulant effect by blocking the absorption of dopamine and norepinephrine (National Institute on Drug Abuse, 2018h). It is approved by the FDA and suppresses tobacco cravings (National Institute on Drug Abuse, 2018h).

Nicotine Replacement Therapy (NRT). There are a variety of nicotine replacement therapies (NRTs), including lozenges and gum as well as a nasal spray and a patch (National Institute on Drug Abuse, 2018h). Each offers a continuous low dose of nicotine that prevents the side effects associated with withdrawal symptoms. Specific to the patch, it is best to combine it with another replacement therapy for best results (National Institute on Drug Abuse, 2018h).

Varenicline. This drug simultaneously stimulates and blocks the nicotine receptors without triggering dopamine to release. The blocking of dopamine reduces cravings and acts as a support in the individual's efforts to stop smoking (National Institute on Drug Abuse, 2018h).

Alcohol Addiction

Acamprosate. This drug can help individuals dependent on alcohol sustain abstinence by acting on the "gamma-aminobutyric acid (GABA) and glutamate neurotransmitter systems" (National Institute on Drug Abuse, 2018h, p. 47). It also reduces withdrawal symptoms such as "insomnia, anxiety, restlessness, and dysphoria" (National Institute on Drug Abuse, 2018h, p. 47).

Disulfiram®. This drug produces a build-up of acetaldehyde when used in conjunction with alcohol, which then causes "flushing, nausea, and palpitations" (National Institute on Drug Abuse, 2018h, p. 47).

Naltrexone®. This drug reduces repeated alcohol abuse by blocking opioid receptors that force alcohol cravings (National Institute on Drug Abuse, 2018h).

Behavioral Therapies

Behavioral treatment approaches increase the odds that individuals who suffer from an addiction can turn their lives around. Choosing and using a drug abuse treatment plan can lead to behaviors that increase sobriety and abstinence as well as help the individual focus on more positive behaviors and attitudes (National Institute on Drug Abuse, 2018h). The proper therapy will also help to build "life skills to handle stressful circumstances and environmental cues that may trigger intense cravings" (National Institute on Drug Abuse, 2018h).

Cognitive-Behavioral Therapy

Cognitive-Behavioral Therapy (CBT) can be used in the treatment of alcohol, cocaine, marijuana, methamphetamine, and nicotine abuse and theorizes "that in the development of maladaptive behavioral patterns like substance abuse, learning processes play a critical role" (National Institute on Drug Abuse, 2018h, p. 49). Through CBT, individuals are able to identify and correct the behaviors that influenced the earlier poor decision making, and using newly learned skills, these individuals are able to eliminate the abuse and other areas that may have caused issues (American Psychological Association, n.d.a).

CBT develops coping strategies to enhance self-control by "exploring the positive and negative consequences of continued drug use, self-monitoring to recognize cravings early and identify situations that might put one at risk for use, and developing strategies for coping with cravings and avoiding those high risk situations" (National Institute on Drug Abuse, 2018h, p. 49).

Contingency Management Interventions/Motivational Incentives

Contingency management involves providing individuals with rewards that reinforce expected behaviors. Tangible incentives have been effective in treating the abuse of alcohol, marijuana, nicotine, opioids, and stimulants (National Institute on Drug Abuse, 2018h).

Voucher-based reinforcement is a process in which a drug-free urine test provides the individual with a voucher that can be exchanged for goods (National Institute on Drug Abuse, 2018h). This is in contrast to the prize incentive management in which individuals earn chances to win prizes through counseling sessions, negative drug tests and meeting goals (National Institute on Drug Abuse, 2018h). In both types of incentives, the value is low to begin but increases as each urine test comes back clear; however, a positive test or lack of meeting goals resets the value.

Community Reinforcement Approach Plus Vouchers (Alcohol, Cocaine, Opioids)

The Community Reinforcement Approach (CRA) Plus Vouchers offers a variety of reinforcers to reward a drug-free life. Using an "intensive 24-week outpatient therapy for treating individuals addicted to cocaine and alcohol" (National

Institute on Drug Abuse, 2018h, p. 53), the therapy goals are two-fold and include maintaining abstinence while learning the necessary life skills and reducing alcohol when used in conjunction with cocaine (Meyers, Roozen & Smith, 2011).

Individual counseling sessions focus on improving family relationships, learning skills to decrease or eliminate the use of drugs, receiving vocational counseling, developing new social networks and enjoyable recreational activities (National Institute on Drug Abuse, 2018h). Similar to other programs, vouchers are given for clean urine samples, increasing with consecutive clean samples, and may be "exchanged for retail goods consistent with a drug-free lifestyle" (National Institute on Drug Abuse, 2018h, p. 53).

Motivational Enhancement Therapy

Motivational Enhancement Therapy (MET) is a counseling approach that assists individuals using alcohol, marijuana, and nicotine in any ambivalence towards treatment and drug use cessation (National Institute on Drug Abuse, 2018h). Beginning with a battery of tests and initial individual treatment sessions, a therapist focuses on feedback, discussion of substance use, and the "eliciting self-motivational statements...[that] build a plan for change" (National Institute on Drug Abuse, 2018h, p. 55). Future sessions center on coping and cessation strategies and encourage a strong commitment to continued change abstinence (National Institute on Drug Abuse, 2018h).

The Matrix Model

The Matrix Model is used with stimulant abusers and aims to teach individuals how to arrive at abstinence and avoid relapse (National Institute on Drug Abuse, 2018h). Treatment sessions promote dignity, self-esteem, and self-worth, while helping the individual find ways to increase positive changes in behaviors (National Institute on Drug Abuse, 2018h). A bond between the therapist and client is critical, as is relationship building with the affected family (National Institute on Drug Abuse, 2018h).

12-Step Facilitation Therapy

Twelve-step facilitation therapy is geared towards individuals who become active members in a new community where abstinence is valued through active engagement (National Institute on Drug Abuse, 2018h). Three main tenets support this program to include acceptance, surrender, and active involvement in the 12-step activities and meetings (National Institute on Drug Abuse, 2018h).

Family Behavior Therapy

Family Behavior Therapy (FBT) combines "behavioral contracting with contingency management" (National Institute on Drug Abuse, 2018h, p. 59) to address substance use problems and other co-occurring issues, such as conduct disorders, depression, family conflict, and unemployment, by combining behavioral contracts with contingency management (National Institute on Drug Abuse, 2018h). Individuals and their family members "develop behavioral goals for preventing substance use" (National Institute on Drug Abuse, 2018h, p. 59), which are then rewarded upon accomplishment.

Multisystemic Therapy

Research demonstrates that adolescents who abuse drugs require different treatments from adults who have similar issues (National Institute on Drug Abuse, 2018h). Children and teens who participate in Multisystemic Therapy (MST) do so in natural settings such as home or school and discuss anti-social behaviors that pushed them towards drugs and alcohol (National Institute on Drug Abuse, 2018h).

Final Thoughts

Individuals begin using drugs for a myriad of reasons and subsequent abuse and addiction lead to harmful consequences regardless of gender and age. With the increasing acceptance and use of opioids, our nation is plunging into an ever-deepening crisis that not only affects public health, but the social and economic welfare of the entire nation. This crisis is growing increasingly complex by the co-involvement of prescription and illicit drugs, which account for 80% of drug-related drug overdoses (Scholl, Seth, Kariisa, Wilson & Baldwin, 2019).

The human brain is the most complex organ in the body, regulating basic bodily functions and interpreting and responding to individual experiences that, in turn, shape thoughts, emotions, and behavior. Drug use affects the brain's communication system and interferes with an individual's reward system, producing euphoric effects that strongly reinforce the behavior of drug use, leading to abuse and addiction. Although each individual has a brain, they are not all the same and not everyone becomes addicted to drugs. The more environmental and biological protective factors an individual has, the less likely they are to develop an addiction. Conversely, the more environmental and biological risk factors associated with an individual, the more susceptible they are to developing an addiction.

Unfortunately, addiction goes beyond drugs, alcohol, and smoking with 1 in 8 individuals being classified as having a behavioral addiction (Substance

Abuse and Mental Health Services Administration, 2019). Although addictions such as sex, shopping, and gaming do not involve substances, like drugs, they do involve activity and/or behavior that provides a means of coping or escaping reality. Fortunately, there are treatments that address all forms of addiction. Pharmacotherapies include the use of methadone and Naltrexone® for opioid addiction, nicotine replacement therapies for tobacco addiction, and Naltrexon®, Acamprosate®, and Disulfiram® for alcohol addiction.

Often, pharmacotherapies are more successful when used in conjunction with behavioral therapies. Cognitive behavioral therapy is successful in enhancing individual self-control and developing effective coping strategies, while contingency management programs and community enhancement therapies work well in rewarding and supporting drug-free behaviors and activities. These, and other behavioral treatment approaches, help engage individuals in drug abuse treatment, while providing them with learned attitudes and behaviors along with lifelong skills to remain drug-free.

Points to Remember

- *Addiction is a chronic, relapsing brain disease characterized by compulsive and difficult to control drug seeking and use despite known harmful consequences.*

- *The brain changes that occur with drug use interfere with an individual's self-control and their ability to resist the intense urges to repetitively use a drug.*

- *Drug addiction risk factors include, but are not limited to genes, gender, easily available drugs, learned environment, financial and familial instability, mental health concerns, and drug route of administration.*

- *Protective factors include, but are not limited to genes, gender, financial stability, learned environment, stable financial and familial environment, and positive relationships at home and within the community.*

- *There are many types of therapies that can address addiction.*

Chapter 2

Depressants, Alcohol & Cannabinoids

Central Nervous System Depressants

Central Nervous System (CNS) depressants "slow brain activity, making them useful for treating anxiety, panic, acute stress reactions, and sleep disorders" (National Institute on Drug Abuse, 2018a, n.p.). Specific examples of CNS depressants include benzodiazepines such as diazepam and clonazepam; non-benzodiazepine sedative hypnotics such as zolpidem; and barbiturates such as phenobarbital and pentobarbital sodium (Guarnotta, 2018; National Institute on Drug Abuse, 2018a).

Physiological Effects

CNS depressants affect an individual's brain by increasing the activity of the neurotransmitter *gamma-aminobutyric acid* (GABA), a chemical that inhibits brain activity (Guarnotta, 2018). According to Hilliard (2019) and National Institute on Drug Abuse (2018a), the use, and misuse, of CNS depressants can cause physiological short-term effects that include but are not limited to dizziness/blackouts and confusion, headaches, memory loss, slow pulse and breathing, and slurred speech. The same sources (Hilliard, 2019; National Institute on Drug Abuse, 2018a), offer a long list of possible long-term effects from CNS depressants that includes but is not limited to addiction/physical dependence, chronic fatigue, weight gain, depression, and suicidal thoughts.

Individuals who abuse CNS depressants are also at greater risk of HIV, hepatitis, and other infectious diseases from shared needles (National Institute on Drug Abuse, 2018a).

Signs of Abuse and Addiction

Individuals can misuse or abuse CNS depressants by taking them in ways that were not intended when prescribed; for example, individuals might take medication prescribed for another individual, mix CNS depressants with other medications, take the medication in a way in which it was not prescribed (e.g., date rape drug, taking a higher dose, taking it more often, snort or inject after crushing), take the medication with the intent to get high, or take CNS depressants to counteract the effects of another drug (National Institute on Drug Abuse, 2018a). In addition to those signs, which may not be visible, individuals who are abusing drugs may show warning signs such as abnormal/secretive behavior, depression and/or mood swings, a decrease in work productivity and/or social interactions, or a lack of motivation (Hilliard, 2019).

Withdrawal and Overdose

Continuous use of CNS depressants can lead to dependence and if suddenly stopped, can lead to withdrawal (Hilliard, 2019; National Institute on Drug Abuse, 2018a). Withdrawal can be sudden and severe, beginning 12-24 hours after the last dose with the most severe symptoms occurring within 24 and 72 hours, although some symptoms may last up to 24 months (Hilliard, 2019). According to Hilliard (2019) and the National Institute on Drug Abuse (2018a) signs of withdrawal may include hypersensitivity to light and sound, body tremors and/or seizures, heart palpitations/increased pulse and blood pressure, severe hallucinations/cravings, and depression/anxiety/panic attacks, just to name a few.

An overdose is a pathologic level of drug toxicity at such a magnitude that it overwhelms normal physiological functioning and a CNS depressant overdose can occur when more than the recommended dose is taken or the medication is combined with another substance, such as alcohol (Guarnotta, 2018; Thomas, 2019). In 2017 alone, approximately 17,000 individuals died from CNS depressant overdoses of which 11,500 deaths were specifically from the misuse of benzodiazepines (National Institute on Drug Abuse for Teens, 2019a).

Although signs of an overdose may differ amongst individuals, general symptoms may include agitation, chest pain, trouble breathing or the inability to breathe, blurred or double vision, agitation, extreme dizziness or weakness (Guarnotta, 2018; Thomas, 2019). Other visible symptoms may include disorientation, confusion, fingernails and lips that appear slightly blue in color, uncoordinated muscle movements or tremors, an altered mental state, unconsciousness, or possibly coma (Guarnotta, 2018; Thomas, 2019).

Rarely, serious complications can occur following a benzodiazepine overdose as a result of respiratory distress, lack of oxygenated blood, or physical trauma caused from any loss of consciousness and may include pneumonia or brain/muscle damage (Guarnotta, 2018; National Institute on Drug Abuse, 2018a). Death from a benzodiazepine overdose is rare when the medication is used alone, although there are certain factors that can put individuals at a higher risk for the serious consequences associated with overdose such as the quantity and frequency of drug dosage, tolerance level and physiological dependence, unexpected interactions from mixing various drugs together, prior incarcerations or overdoses/suicide attempts (Thomas, 2019; Guarnotta, 2018).

Alcohol

Ethanol, or alcohol, is produced through the "fermentation process of yeast, sugars, and starches" (Centers for Disease Control and Prevention, 2018a, n.p.). All alcoholic beverages contain ethanol and are typically divided into three categories to include (1) wine, which is fermented from grapes and other fruits; and (2) distilled spirits, which are made from sugar sources such as fruits or grains, "that are fermented and then distilled in a heating and cooling process that concentrates the alcohol" (Responsible Drinking, n.d., n.p.); and (3) beer, which is made from sprouted barley and "roasted into malt...cooked with water, fermented with yeast, and flavored with the flowers of the hops plant" (Responsible Drinking, n.d., n.p.).

Despite alcohol's depressant effects and it being the third leading preventable cause of death, "86.3 percent of individuals ages 18 or older reported that they drank alcohol at some point in their lifetime, 70 percent reported that they drank in the past year, and 55.3 percent reported that they drank in the past month" (National Institute on Alcohol Abuse and Alcoholism, 2019a, n.p.). In addition, of those in the 12-20-year-old age bracket, or approximately 7.1 million individuals, drank alcohol in the last month (National Institute on Alcohol Abuse and Alcoholism, 2019a).

Physiological Effects

The effects of alcohol can vary depending on how much, how often, and how quickly alcohol is consumed by an individual, as well as how much food was consumed prior to drinking, age, sex, race, physical condition, health status, use of drugs or prescription medications, and family history (Brande, 2017; Centers for Disease Control and Prevention, 2018a). Although drinking itself may not be an issue, drinking in excess can cause a variety of effects and have varied consequences (National Institute on Alcohol Abuse and Alcoholism, 2019b).

Alcohol interferes with many systems found within the human body and is rapidly absorbed from the stomach and small intestine into the bloodstream. As the liver can only metabolize a small amount of alcohol at a time, the excess circulates throughout the body, making the intensity of its effects directly proportional to the amount consumed (National Institute on Alcohol Abuse and Alcoholism, 2019b; Zakhari, 2006).

Significant areas of the brain will sustain damage from alcohol consumption including the cerebral cortex, which is largely responsible for higher brain functions such as problem solving and decision making, the hippocampus, which is important for memory and learning, and the cerebellum, which controls movement coordination (National Institute on Alcohol Abuse and Alcoholism, 2019b).

Consuming alcohol cannot only damage the brain, but most body organs as well. Heart damage can occur, such as stretching and drooping of the heart muscle, irregular heartbeat, stroke, and high blood pressure (National Institute on Alcohol Abuse and Alcoholism, 2019b). Excessive drinking can lead to inflammation of the liver and a wide range of issues including fatty liver, alcohol hepatitis, fibrosis, and cirrhosis (National Institute on Alcohol Abuse and Alcoholism, 2019b; Zakhari, 2006).

Extensive research studies have also found alcohol to be a strong carcinogen and that there is a strong connection between alcohol consumption and cancer; for example, alcohol has been found to be the primary cause of liver cancer and 43-47% of liver disease deaths being caused by alcohol (National Institute on Alcohol Abuse and Alcoholism, 2019b). Studies indicate that individuals who consume 3.5 or more drinks per day are at a 2-3 times greater risk for developing head and neck cancers, particularly of the oral cavity, pharynx, and larynx. This risk becomes even higher with concurrent alcohol and tobacco use (Freedman, Schatzin, Leitzmann, Hollenbeck & Abnet, 2007).

As reported by the National Cancer Institute (2018), a collection of epidemiologic studies have found that an increase in alcohol consumption is positively correlated to an increased risk of breast cancer in women. Women who drank more than 3 alcoholic beverages a day were 1.5 times more likely to develop breast cancer than those who did not consume alcohol (National Cancer Institute, 2018). Perhaps more concerning, those same studies found that there was a 12 percent increase in the risk of breast cancer in women who consumed just "10 grams of alcohol per day" (National Institute on Alcohol Abuse and Alcoholism, n.d.a, n.p.).

Short and Long Term Effects

As alcohol enters the bloodstream, it immediately causes changes to the individual and the outward effects can appear in as few as ten minutes (National Institutes of Health: National Institute on Alcohol Abuse and Alcoholism, n.d.b). As the blood alcohol concentration (BAC) increases, so does the level of impairment and possible negative effects (National Institutes of Health: National Institute on Alcohol Abuse and Alcoholism, n.d.b). The effects from an abuse of alcohol may include confusion/concentration/memory issues, motor impairments, reduced inhibitions, and slurred speech (National Institutes of Health: National Institute on Alcohol Abuse and Alcoholism, n.d.b). More serious bodily issues include alcohol use disorder, breathing issues, B1 deficiency/Wernicke-Korsakoff syndrome, and risk for some cancers, (National Cancer Institute, 2018). Coma and death also stand out as real possibilities when alcoholism goes untreated (National Institutes of Health: National Institute on Alcohol Abuse and Alcoholism, n.d.b).

Sociological Effects

Not only are there physiological effects to excessive alcohol consumption, but drinking in excess can also lead to numerous sociological effects and consequences; for example, more than 10% of children in the United States live with a parent that has trouble with alcohol, a risk factor in whether children will be subsequent users of alcohol (Lander et al., 2013; Reuters, 2012). Children of alcoholics may be subjected to a parent's unpredictable and unreliable negative and/or violent behavior, including abuse (Lander et al., 2013). Financial aid familial strain can also occur as an alcoholic may lose their employment and lose interest in relationships (Okhifun, 2010).

Research shows that teenage use of alcohol interferes with normal adolescent brain development and contributes to a variety of acute consequences, such as injuries, sexual assaults, risky and/or violent behavior, car accidents, and suicide/homicide (Fleming, 2015; Hiller-Sturmhofel & Swartzwelder, n.d.; Squeglia, Jacobus & Tapert, 2009).

The number of incidences with underage college drinking, those students between the ages of 18 and 24, each year are staggering with more than 1,800 individuals dying from unintentional alcohol-related injuries (National Institutes of Health: National Institute on Alcohol Abuse and Alcoholism, 2019a). Students who have been assaulted by another student under the influence of alcohol totals another 696,000, while 97,000 students have experienced date rape or sexual assault due to excessive drinking (National Institute on Alcohol Abuse and Alcoholism, 2019a). It is not surprising then, that college students have academic issues such as missed class time to include falling behind in assignments, poor academic performance, and low grades (National Institutes of Health: National Institute on Alcohol Abuse and Alcoholism, 2019a).

Alcohol Use Disorder

Alcohol use disorder (AUD) is a "chronic relapsing brain disease characterized by compulsive alcohol use, loss of control over alcohol intake, and a negative emotional state when not using" (National Institute on Alcohol Abuse and Alcoholism, n.d.c, n.p.). Approximately 16 million people in the United States have been diagnosed with AUD, including 623,000 adolescents between the ages of 12 and 17 (National Institute on Alcohol Abuse and Alcoholism, n.d.c).

According to the DSM-5 (American Psychiatric Association, 2013), individuals must meet two of 11 different criteria in any 12-month period to be diagnosed with AUD. The designation of mild (2-3), moderate (4-5), or severe (6+) correlates to the number of criteria met (American Psychiatric Association, 2013; National Institute on Alcohol Abuse and Alcoholism, n.d.c). To decide if AUD is present, the American Psychiatric Association (2013) suggests considering if

1. Alcohol has been taken in larger amounts or over a longer period than was intended.

2. There is a persistent desire or unsuccessful efforts to cut down or control alcohol use.

3. A great deal of time is spent participating in activities necessary to obtain alcohol, use alcohol, or recover from its effects.

4. There is a strong desire, craving or urge to drink alcohol.

5. Recurrent alcohol use results in a failure to fulfill major role obligations at work, school, or home.

6. Continued alcohol use despite having persistent or recurrent social or interpersonal problems caused or exacerbated by the effects of alcohol.

7. Important social, occupational, or recreational activities are given up or reduced due to excessive alcohol use.

8. Recurrent alcohol use in situations where it is physically hazardous.

9. Alcohol use is continued despite knowledge of having a persistent or recurrent physical or psychological problem that is likely to have been caused or exacerbated by alcohol.

10. Tolerance, as defined by a need for markedly increased amounts of alcohol to achieve intoxication or desired effect or a markedly diminished effect with continued use of the same amount of alcohol.

11. Characteristic withdrawal symptoms for alcohol or alcohol (or a closely related substance, such as a benzodiazepine) is taken to relieve or avoid withdrawal symptoms.

Withdrawal and Delirium Tremens

Symptoms of alcohol withdrawal occur with the sudden cessation of alcohol use subsequent to regular excessive drinking (Harvard Medical School, 2019). Symptoms can range from mild to severe, with severe withdrawal symptoms occurring between 1-3 days after drinking is stopped (Jesse et al., 2016). Common withdrawal symptoms are grouped into four categories to include autonomic symptoms, such as tachycardia or nausea/vomiting; motor symptoms, such as tremors or seizures; awareness symptoms, such as insomnia or disorientation; and psychiatric symptoms, such as hallucinations or combativeness (Jesse et al., 2016).

Delirium Tremens

With heavy, long-term drinking, the brain is continually exposed to the depressant effect of alcohol (Rahman & Paul, 2019). As a result, the brain adjusts its own chemistry to compensate for the consistent depressive inputs it receives (Harvard Medical School, 2019; Rahman & Paul, 2019). Delirium tremens are the result of the brain's inability to recalibrate without alcohol; thus, creating confusion and volatility in the regulation of circulation, breathing, heart rate, and blood pressure (Harvard Medical School, 2019). With so many bodily circuits running amuck, the "risk for heart attack, stroke or death" (Harvard Medical School, 2019, n.p.) increases dramatically.

Approximately 1 out of 20 individuals who withdraw from excessive and heavy alcohol use experience the most severe, and potentially fatal, symptoms of alcohol withdrawal known as delirium tremens (Harvard Medical School, 2019). Symptoms of delirium tremens typically begin within two to three days after the last drink and peak within four to five days; however, it is not unusual for them to be delayed by a week or more (Harvard Medical School, 2019). Common symptoms include "confusion, disorientation, stupor or loss of consciousness, nervous or angry behavior, irrational beliefs, soaking sweats, sleep disturbances and hallucinations" (Harvard Medical School, 2019, n.p.).

Post-Acute Withdrawal Syndrome (PAWS)

Prolonged side effects are not uncommon and may last as little as several weeks or as much as a year (Galbicsek, 2019; Maclaren, 2018). The exact number, combination, and timing of symptoms can differ for each individual based on physical characteristics and the amount and frequency of alcohol abuse (Galbicsek, 2019; Maclaren, 2018). While the list of symptoms is long, it may include emotional outbursts, sensitivity to stress and anxiety and delayed reflexes; however, more severe side effects may be noticeable as well and might include depression, tremors, seizures, and cognitive impairment (Galbicsek, 2019; Maclaren, 2018).

Overdose

An alcohol overdose occurs when there is an excessive amount of alcohol in the bloodstream and the areas of the brain controlling basic life-support functions begin to shut down (National Institutes of Health: National Institute on Alcohol Abuse and Alcoholism, 2019b; Brande, 2017). Factors that can influence the level of toxicity in an individual may include tolerance to drinking/binge drinking, rate of consumption/tolerance, body mass, and a lack of understanding with personal limits (Brande, 2017).

Individuals, particularly teenagers and college-age young adults, who engage in binge drinking, a pattern of drinking that brings blood alcohol concentration to .08 percent or higher, are at increased risk of an overdose (National Institute on Alcohol Abuse and Alcoholism, 2018). Research found that overdosing on alcohol is fairly common, with 6 people dying per day from alcohol poisoning (Brande, 2017). According to the National Institutes of Health: National Institute on Alcohol Abuse and Alcoholism (2019b) symptoms of alcohol overdose may include low body temperatures/bluish skin tone/paleness, clammy skin/slow heart rate/slow breathing, vomiting/seizures or mental confusion.

Marijuana

Marijuana, the most commonly used illicit drug, is the dried leaves, flowers, stems, and seeds from the *Cannabis sativa* or *Cannabis indica* plant, which contains the mind-altering chemical THC (National Institute on Drug Abuse, 2014a; National Institute on Drug Abuse, 2019a; National Institute on Drug Abuse for Teens, 2019b). Marijuana can be smoked via joints, pipes, bongs, blunts, can be mixed in food to form edibles, or brewed into tea (National Institute on Drug Abuse, 2019a; National Institute on Drug Abuse for Teens, 2019b).

Physiological Effects

Marijuana passes quickly from the lungs into the bloodstream, which then carries the chemical to the brain and other bodily organs. THC over activates specific brain cell receptors, causing the feeling of being high and stimulating the release of dopamine in the reward centers of the brain, reinforcing the behavior (National Institute on Drug Abuse, 2019a; National Institute on Drug Abuse for Teens, 2019b). Once an individual inhales marijuana vapors, their heart rate will increase, the eyes become bloodshot due to an expansion of the blood vessels, and the bronchia relax and become enlarged (National Institute on Drug Abuse for Teens, 2019b). In addition to these more common effects, those who smoke marijuana may also find they have an altered sense of time, changes in mood and problem-solving abilities, impaired thinking/memory/body movements, as well as anxiety/delusions/psychosis/hallucinations (National Institute on Drug Abuse, 2014a; National Institute on Drug Abuse, 2019a; National Institute on Drug Abuse for Teens, 2019b).

Physical Effects

The physical effects of marijuana inhalation and continued use include lung irritation, nausea/vomiting, increased heart rate, dehydration and lung infections/disease/cancer (National Institute on Drug Abuse, 2014a; National Institute on Drug Abuse, 2019a).

Sociological Effects

Students who smoke marijuana may have poor academic performance or drop out of school altogether, while adults may find they have poor peer and family relations or reduced overall life satisfaction (National Institute on Drug Abuse for Teens, 2019b).

Medical Marijuana

Medical marijuana refers to the use of the plant parts to treat the symptoms of illness such as nausea, pain, and inflammation, as well as mental health issues such as anxiety (National Institute on Drug Abuse, 2019a). Certain states have recognized marijuana as legal in small amounts; however, the U.S. Food and Drug Administration (FDA) has not approved the marijuana plant as medicine (National Institute on Drug Abuse, 2019a). Research on cannabinoids, specifically THC and CBD, has led to two FDA-approved medications, including a CBD-based liquid medication for the treatment of two forms of severe childhood epilepsy, Dravet syndrome and Lennox-Gastaut syndrome (National Institute on Drug Abuse, 2019a; National Institute on Drug Abuse for Teens, 2019b).

Marijuana Use Disorder

Marijuana use can lead to the development of a marijuana use disorder and addiction (National Institute on Drug Abuse, 2019e; National Institute on Drug Abuse for Teens, 2019b). Research found that 30% of individuals who use marijuana have some degree of marijuana use disorder and those who began using prior to age 18 are 4-7 times more likely to develop a marijuana use disorder than adults (National Institute on Drug Abuse, 2019a). In 2015, 138,000 individuals voluntarily sought treatment for marijuana disorder; however, that is much less than the 4.0 million of those who met the criteria for the syndrome (National Institute on Drug Abuse, 2019a).

Individuals who suffer from dependence and a marijuana use disorder may feel mild withdrawal symptoms when they stop using. Symptoms of withdrawal can last for several days to a few weeks and include irritability, sleeplessness, lack of appetite, cravings, restlessness, weight loss, anxiety, and drug cravings (National Institute on Drug Abuse for Teens, 2019b).

Final Thoughts

Central nervous system depressants, alcohol, and marijuana all change the normal functioning of an individual's brain and can lead to lasting changes and severe side effects. While central nervous system depressants and marijuana, to an extent, are useful in combating physical and mental health illnesses, individuals may be at greater risk for other conditions.

Although alcohol is legal, socially acceptable, and widely consumed, it has the propensity to be abused and often results in addiction, which can lead to long-lasting health and sociological consequences. Like alcohol, the social acceptability and medical use of marijuana is on the rise, but with increased use comes an increase in side effects and potential for abuse and addiction.

Evidence shows that while there are physical, mental and even social benefits to these drugs, the effects of abuse and addiction can outweigh these at a moment's notice, particularly for adolescents and young adults, whose brain chemistry and ability to function in the world can be permanently affected.

Points to Remember

- *The number of individuals under the age of 18 who have consumed alcohol at some point in their lifetime is staggering and many do not see it as an issue; therefore, they do not seek help.*

- *Research demonstrated a strong correlation between alcohol and cancer.*

- *Every year, college students die as a result of alcohol-related unintentional injuries, many are assaulted by another student who has been drinking or experience alcohol-related sexual assault or date rape.*

- *At least a third of individuals who use marijuana have a marijuana use disorder and individuals who start using before are 18 are 4-7 times more likely than their adult counterparts to develop a marijuana use disorder.*

Chapter 3

Stimulants, Psychotherapeutic and Other Prescription Medications

Nicotine

Nicotine is both a sedating and stimulating chemical found in the dried and fermented leaves of the tobacco plant but can also be produced synthetically (Felman, 2018; Psychology Today, 2019a). Tobacco can be smoked, chewed or sniffed in products such as cigarettes, cigars, pipes, snuff, and dip (National Institute on Drug Abuse, 2020; National Institute on Drug Abuse for Teens, 2020).

Surveys indicate that an estimated 63.4 million individuals, ages 12 and over, use tobacco products with 51.3 million choosing to smoke cigarettes (National Institute on Drug Abuse, 2020). It has also been found that 25% of the American population suffering from mental health disorders account for 40% of the cigarettes smoked (National Institute on Drug Abuse, 2020).

Physiological Effects

The average smoker will ingest 1–2 milligrams of nicotine in a single cigarette (about 10 puffs over five minutes) and these individuals smoke approximately a pack a day, which results in over "200 hits of nicotine to the brain" (National Institute on Drug Abuse 2020, p. 6). After inhaling tobacco smoke, nicotine rapidly enters the bloodstream and reaches the brain within 8-20 seconds, stimulating the adrenal glands, resulting in the release of epinephrine, which then stimulates the body to release glucose as well as increase blood sugar, heart rate, breathing activity, and blood pressure (Felman, 2018).

Nicotine causes the release of dopamine and norepinephrine in the brain, similar to heroin and cocaine, causing feelings of euphoria, relaxation, and raised alertness as well as improved memory and concentration (Felman, 2018; National Institute on Drug Abuse, 2020). Repeated exposure can alter sensitivity to dopamine in the brain and lead to changes in the brain circuits that are involved in learning, stress, and self-control. These long-term brain changes can thus result in addiction (Martin, 2019; Psychology Today, 2019a).

The exact amount of nicotine that enters an individual's body depends on the type of tobacco being used, whether the tobacco is inhaled, whether a filter is used and what type (Martin, 2019). Tobacco products that are chewed, placed inside the mouth or snorted, versus smoked, have been found to release higher amounts of nicotine into an individual's body (Felman, 2018).

There are a plethora of short- and long-term effects to smoking, chewing, or inhaling tobacco. A few notable short-term effects include lightheadedness, nausea and vomiting, blood restriction, increase in blood pressure and heartburn (Felman, 2018; Martin, 2019; National Institute on Drug Abuse, 2020). Long-term effects are more disturbing and include, but are not limited to joint pain, lung disease, pneumonia, and an increased risk of cancer, stroke and Alzheimer's disease, not to mention death (Felman, 2018; Martin, 2019; National Institute on Drug Abuse, 2020).

Research has demonstrated that "smokers aged 60 and older have a twofold increase in mortality [when compared to individuals of the same age] who have never smoked, dying an estimated 6 years earlier" (National Institute on Drug Abuse, 2020, p. 10). Studies have shown that 80-90% of lung cancer cases have been caused by cigarette smoking, which is the primary "cause of cancer death for both men and women" (National Institute on Drug Abuse, 2020, p. 10).

Addiction and Withdrawal

Nicotine has been proven to be highly addictive and the majority of smokers would like to stop smoking although only 6% are able to quit in any given year (Centers for Disease Control and Prevention, 2011). Due to nicotine's highly addictive nature, individuals who regularly consume nicotine can experience a bevy of withdrawal symptoms with sudden cessation that include, but are not limited to cravings, cognitive deficits, chest tightness, moodiness, and headache (Felman, 2018; Martin, 2019; National Institute on Drug Abuse, 2020; Psychology Today, 2019). Numerous behavioral factors can affect the severity of withdrawal symptoms. For example, the feel, smell, and sight of a cigarette and the ritual of obtaining, handling, lighting, and smoking the cigarette are associated with the pleasurable effects of smoking, intensifying withdrawal symptoms (National Institute on Drug Abuse 2020; Psychology Today, 2019a).

Tobacco Use Disorder

Individuals diagnosed with a tobacco use disorder exhibit a pattern of daily tobacco use that leads to clinically significant impairment or distress within a 12-month period (Psychology Today, 2019a). Two of the following symptoms must be met for an individual to be diagnosed with tobacco use disorder:

- *Tobacco is taken in larger dosages and/or for a longer period of time than intended*

- *There is a persistent desire and/or failed attempts to reduce tobacco use*

- *A large amount of time goes into procuring or using tobacco*

- *An overwhelming desire or urge to use tobacco*

- *The inability, due to tobacco use, to maintain obligations related to job, school, or home life*

- *Continued tobacco use in the face of social/interpersonal problems that result from, or are made worse by, the use of the stimulant*

- *Tobacco use becomes prioritized to such an extent that social, occupational, and recreational activities are either given up on completely or are reduced drastically*

- *Tobacco use occurs even in situations where it becomes physically hazardous*

- *Use of tobacco continues even though one knows the physical and psychological risks and problems associated with it*

- *A considerable increase in the amount of tobacco is needed to achieve the desired effect, or the same amount of tobacco no longer produces the desired effect*

- *Withdrawal symptoms characteristic of tobacco use are present, or tobacco is taken to relieve or avoid withdrawal symptoms*
  (Psychology Today, 2019a, n.p.).

E-Cigarettes and Vaporizers

Electronic cigarettes are battery-operated devices individuals use to inhale an aerosol that contains nicotine, flavorings, and other chemicals to the lungs in the form of vapor instead of smoke (National Institute on Drug Abuse, 2020). E-cigarette devices contain a cartridge, or reservoir, that holds a flavored liquid nicotine solution, a heating element, a power source, and a mouthpiece. When the device is puffed on, the heating device is activated and vaporizes the liquid into a vapor that an individual can inhale (National Institute on Drug Abuse, 2020).

These devices have become the most commonly used form of tobacco among youth in the United States due to their ease of availability, alluring advertisements, various e-liquid flavors, and the belief that they are safer than smoking cigarettes (National Institute on Drug Abuse, 2020). One study found that 1 in 4 teens use e-cigarettes for dripping, a practice in which vapors are produced and inhaled by placing e-liquid drops directly onto heated atomizer coils (National Institute on Drug Abuse for Teens, 2020).

Research has also demonstrated that students who had used e-cigarettes in or prior to 9th grade were more likely to start smoking cigarettes within the next year and any students who had used e-cigarettes in the last month were 7 times more likely to smoke cigarettes (National Institute on Drug Abuse, 2020; National Institute on Drug Abuse for Teens, 2020). Additional studies have shown that approximately 50% of current adult cigarette smokers have used an e-cigarette device at some point, while 21% currently use a device (National Institute on Drug Abuse, 2020). Interestingly, 10% of device users reported never smoking previously to their use of an e-cigarette device (National Institute on Drug Abuse for Teens, 2020).

Risks

Using an e-cigarette exposes an individual's lungs to a variety of chemicals that are either added to the e-liquid or produced during the heating/vaporizing process. Studies have found that the vapors produced by the devices contain known carcinogens, toxic chemicals, and toxic metal nanoparticles from the actual device itself (National Institute on Drug Abuse, 2019e).

Recently, the Food and Drug Administration has alerted public consumers on the numerous reports of serious lung illnesses associated with vaping, including several deaths. Although no single substance has been identified in relation to the reported illnesses, federal agencies have identified vaping products containing THC, the main psychotropic ingredient in marijuana (National Institute on Drug Abuse, 2019e).

Secondhand Smoke

Individuals who do not smoke but are exposed to secondhand smoke are at increased risk for disease (National Institute on Drug Abuse for Teens, 2020). Studies have found that approximately 58 million Americans are regularly exposed to secondhand smoke each year and more than 42,000 nonsmokers die per year from diseases caused by exposure to secondhand smoke (National Institute on Drug Abuse for Teens, 2020).

Individuals exposed to secondhand smoke are at an increased risk for lung cancer by 20% to 30% and approximately 7,300 nonsmoker deaths from lung cancer have occurred due to secondhand smoke exposure (National Institute on Drug Abuse for Teens, 2020). Similarly, a nonsmoker's heart disease risk is increased by 25%-30% and secondhand smoke has contributed to approximately 34,000 heart disease deaths (National Institute on Drug Abuse for Teens, 2020).

Overdose

Although overdosing on nicotine is uncommon, it is possible, particularly for young children who accidentally chew on nicotine gum or swallow e-cigarette liquid. Symptoms of a nicotine overdose can include difficulty breathing, vomiting, fainting, headache, weakness, and increased or decreased heart rate (Martin, 2019; National Institute on Drug Abuse, 2020).

Prescription Medications/Opioids

Prescription medications include opioid pain relievers, such as OxyContin® and Vicodin®, anti-anxiety sedatives, such as Valium® and Xanax®, and ADHD stimulants, such as Adderall® and Ritalin® (National Institute on Drug Abuse, 2019b; National Institute on Drug Abuse, 2019c; National Institute on Drug Abuse, 2018a). Specifically, prescription opioids are medications that are chemically similar to endorphins and can be found naturally in the seed pod of the opium poppy plant or created synthetically (National Institute on Drug Abuse, 2019b). Prescription opioids usually come in pill or liquid form and are given to treat severe pain, chronic pain, serious sports injuries, or cancer (National Institute on Drug Abuse, 2019b; National Institute on Drug Abuse, 2018a).

Misuse

Prescription opioids and other medications are commonly misused to self-treat medical issues or abused solely for the purpose of getting high or improve performance (National Institute on Drug Abuse, 2019; National Institute on Drug Abuse, 2014a). Research found that in 2017, an estimated 18 million people misused such medications at least once in the past year (National Institute on Drug Abuse, 2018a). Prescription medications can also be abused by an individual when they take another individual's prescription medication, when they take their own medication in a way other than prescribed or in a way that it was not meant to be taken, and by mixing it with alcohol or other drugs (National Institute on Drug Abuse, 2019b; National Institute on Drug Abuse, 2019c).

Physiological Effects

Each class of prescription drugs works differently in the brain and some can cause actions that are similar to those of illegal drugs; for example, prescription opioid pain medications bind to molecules on the opioid receptors of the brain, which are the same receptors that respond to heroin, as well as in the spinal cord to reduce the intensity of pain-signal perception (National Institute on Drug Abuse, 2019c).

When taken, opioids affect the reward circuit of the brain, resulting in a euphoric high feeling and a flooding of the reward circuit of the brain with dopamine. This surge encourages the individual to continue the pleasurable experience with the unhealthy behavior of taking drugs, thus leading to addiction (National Institute on Drug Abuse, 2019b; National Institute on Drug Abuse, 2018a).

Short- & Long-Term Effects

As with most drugs, the list of short- and long-term effects is long. What follows are just a few examples of what may happen to an individual who abuses opioids. Short-term effects may include drowsiness, mental confusion, or slowing heart rate; while long-term effects include depression, addiction, and overdose (National Institute on Drug Abuse, 2019c).

Opioid Intoxication

Opioid intoxication occurs when "recent exposure to an opioid causes significant problematic behavioral or psychological changes" (Psychology Today, 2019b). Symptoms of intoxication can be both psychological or physical and may include:

- *initial euphoria followed by apathy*
- *a strong sense of unease*
- *unintentional and purposeless movement*
- *slowed cognition and movement*
- *impaired judgment*
- *pupil constriction or dilation*
- *slurred speech*
- *impairment in attention or memory*
- *drowsiness*
- *coma*

    (Psychology Today, 2019b, n.p.).

Addiction/Opioid Use Disorder

The use and misuse of prescription drugs over a long period of time can change brain function causing physical dependence, and thus lead to a substance use disorder (addiction) (National Institute on Drug Abuse, 2019b). To be clinically diagnosed with the disorder, an individual must experience a pattern of opioid use that results in impairment or distress due to at least two of the following within the previous year:

- Taking larger dosages and/or taking opioids for a longer period of time than intended

- Wanting or desiring to reduce opioid use, or making unsuccessful efforts to reduce use

- Spending a large amount of time procuring, using, or recovering from the effects of opioids

- An overwhelming desire or urge to use opioids

- The inability, due to opioid use, to meet employment, school, or domestic responsibilities

- Continued use of opioids despite social/interpersonal problems that result from, or are made worse by, the use of opioids

- Prioritizing opioid use to the extent that social, occupational, and recreational activities are completely given up or are drastically reduced

- Using opioids in physically hazardous situations

- Opioid use continues despite the knowledge that use causes or exacerbates physical and psychological problems

- Tolerance develops in the form of either of the following:
  - o Intoxication requires greater amounts of opioid use
  - o The same dose of opioid over the same amount of time results in weaker effects

- Withdrawal develops in the form of either of the following:
  - o Individuals display characteristics of Opioid Withdrawal Syndrome
  - o Symptoms of withdrawal diminish as a result of the use of opioids (or similar substances)

(Psychology Today, 2019b; American Psychiatric Association, 2013).

Withdrawal and Overdose

Opioid withdrawal can take as few as 6 hours to begin and can last as long as four to six days (Psychology Today, 2019b). As with other drugs and substances, the list of possible symptoms is long and may include anxiety, muscle and bone pain, nausea/vomiting, leg spasms, and increased sensitivity to pain (National Institute on Drug Abuse, 2019; National Institute on Drug Abuse for Teens, 2019c; Psychology Today, 2019b; National Institute on Drug Abuse, 2018a).

Evidence has shown that more than 50% of the drug overdose deaths in the United States each year are caused by prescription drug misuse (Center for Disease Control and Prevention, 2019d). In 2017 alone, more than 33,800 individuals died from a prescription drug overdose (Center for Disease Control and Prevention, 2019d). Signs of prescription opioid overdose include, but are not limited to blue lips/fingernails, shaking, vomiting, brain damage and coma/death (Center for Disease Control and Prevention, 2019d).

Stimulants

Prescription stimulants are medications, such as dextroamphetamine (Dexedrine®), dextroamphetamine/amphetamine combination product (Adderall®), and methylphenidate (Ritalin®, Concerta®) that affect both the autonomic and central nervous systems as a means to increase alertness, attention, and energy and are typically used to treat narcolepsy and attention-deficit/hyperactivity disorder (Cherry, 2019; National Institute on Drug Abuse for Teens, 2019c; National Institute on Drug Abuse, 2018a). Data reflecting usage trends from 2015 and 2016 revealed that "approximately 6.5% (or 16 million) U.S. adults used prescription stimulants appropriately...2.1% (or 5 million) misused...[these drugs]...and .02% (or 0.4 million) [U.S. adults] had prescription stimulant use disorders" (National Institute on Drug Abuse, 2019b).

Physiological Effects

Prescription stimulants increase brain activity by boosting the dopamine, which reinforces gratification, and norepinephrine, which affects "blood pressure, heart rate, and respiration" (National Institute on Drug Abuse, 2018a, p. 15). Individuals taking prescription stimulants may feel short-term side effects that include but are not limited to an increase in blood pressure/heart rate/breathing, a decrease in blood flow/blood sugar and a feeling of euphoria (National Institute on Drug Abuse, 2018a). In higher doses, short-term effects are likely to include irregular heartbeat, heart failure, and stroke, among others (National Institute on Drug Abuse, 2018a). Long-term effects may include extreme anger, heart issues, psychosis and/or paranoia (National Institute on Drug Abuse for Teens, 2019c).

Misuse

The majority of prescription stimulants are ingested orally. When an individual misuses this medication, it is often taken in a manner that is non-prescribed (National Institute on Drug Abuse, 2018a). This may include crushing and snorting the powdery substance or turning it into a liquid that might be injected directly into the vein, or simply taking a higher dose orally (National Institute on Drug Abuse, 2018a).

Addiction & Withdrawal

Misuse and long-term use of a prescription stimulant can lead to a substance use disorder and addiction (Compton, Han, Blanco, Johnson & Jones, 2018). When the stimulant is stopped, withdrawal symptoms can occur and may include fatigue, depression, suicidal ideations, anxiety, and drug cravings (Compton et al., 2018; National Institute on Drug Abuse, 2018a).

Overdose

An overdose on prescription stimulants can occur and is evidenced by early symptoms such as hallucinations, irregular heartbeat, and nausea/vomiting and late onset symptoms such as convulsions, coma, and death (Compton et al., 2018; National Institute on Drug Abuse, 2018a).

Cocaine

Cocaine is a powerful "addictive stimulant drug made from the leaves of the coca plant native to South America" (National Institute on Drug Abuse for Teens, 2019d, n.p.). As an illegal drug, it takes the form of a fine, white, crystal powder that is often mixed with other substances such as synthetic opioids such as Fentanyl® or amphetamines such as Adderall® (American Addiction Centers, 2020a; National Institute on Drug Abuse for Teens, 2019d; National Institute on Drug Abuse, 2018c). This powder can then be snorted through the nose, rubbed into the gumline, or dissolved and injected directly into the bloodstream (National Institute on Drug Abuse for Teens, 2019d; National Institute on Drug Abuse, 2018c). Cocaine can also be processed to make a rock crystal, often referred to as crack, that is then heated to produce vapors that are inhaled into the lungs (crack) (National Institute on Drug Abuse for Teens, 2019d; National Institute on Drug Abuse, 2018c).

Approximately 2 million U.S. citizens used cocaine in 2018, a number that is up by more than half a million since 2011 (Ungar, 2019). Fourteen thousand Americans died from a cocaine overdose in 2017, that number was up 34% from the prior year and much of that increase is due to cocaine being mixed with

Fentanyl® (Ungar, 2019). The largest group of users are adults between the ages of 45 to 54 (Ungar, 2019).

Physiological Effects

Dopamine, a naturally occurring chemical in the brain, is increased with the use of cocaine causing a brick wall effect to occur between two nerve cells, rendering them unable to communicate (National Institute on Drug Abuse, 2018c). As users become less sensitive to the effects of using cocaine, individuals must use more and more to receive the same high and also to eliminate the possibility of withdrawal symptoms (National Institute on Drug Abuse, 2018c).

Short- and Long-Term Effects

The effects of cocaine and their intensity appear immediately and disappear within a few minutes to an hour depending on the method of use; for example, the injection of cocaine causes a high that is shorter in duration; however, it begins quicker and may be stronger in feeling, whereas snorting cocaine will result in a longer-lasting high of up to 30 minutes (American Addiction Centers, 2020a; National Institute on Drug Abuse, 2018c). When mixed with other drugs or alcohol, the side effects may be more noticeable as each drug/alcohol has its own outward signs.

The short-term effects of cocaine include but are not limited to profuse happiness and mental clarity, paranoia, unpredictable behaviors, nausea, and weight loss (National Institute on Drug Abuse, 2018c). Depending on the type of use, the long-term effects vary and may include nosebleeds and issues with swallowing for those who snort cocaine, bowel deterioration for those who swallow cocaine, respiratory distress and asthma for those who smoke cocaine, and blood-borne diseases and collapsed veins for those who inject cocaine (National Institute on Drug Abuse, 2018c).

Addiction/Withdrawal

Repeated use of cocaine causes the reward circuits of the brain to adapt to the extra dopamine caused by the drug and steadily becomes less sensitive to its effects. As a result, addiction ensues and individuals must take stronger and more frequent doses to feel the same effect as they did from the initial dose or to relieve the effects of withdrawal such as mood swings, cravings (food and drug), insomnia and irritability, just to name a few (American Addiction Centers, 2020a).

Overdose

Overdose by cocaine can be intentional or unintentional and death can occur at any time. Consuming alcohol or mixing cocaine with another illicit drug increases the risk of overdose (American Addiction Centers, 2020a; National Institute on Drug Abuse, 2018c). The most common and serious consequences of overdose include seizures, hallucinations, anxiety, heart attack, and stroke (National Institute on Drug Abuse, 2018c).

Steroids and Other Appearance and Performance Enhancing Drugs

Anabolic-androgenic steroids, a specific class of appearance and performance-enhancing drugs (APEDs), are synthetic variations of the male sex hormone testosterone that are most often used by males to improve performance by building muscle mass or to enhance athletic performance (Davis, 2018; National Institute on Drug Abuse, 2018d; Preiato, 2019).

Misuse

Males between the ages of 20 and 40 most often misuse APEDs, although there are outliers (National Institute on Drug Abuse, 2018d). Dosages are often 10 to 100 times greater than prescribed (National Institute on Drug Abuse, 2018d). These individuals typically consume APEDs in one of four different ways to include oral consumption in pill form, injection into muscles, pellets placed just under the skin, or application to the skin as a gel or cream (Davis, 2018; National Institute on Drug Abuse, 2018d).

In the first pattern of misuse, 'cycling' refers to individuals who take multiple doses of a steroid for a specific period of time, stop for a designated amount of time, and then restart use (National Institute on Drug Abuse, 2018d). The second pattern involves 'stacking' or combining of two or more different steroids and mixing oral and/or injectable types (National Institute on Drug Abuse, 2018d). Those who choose to 'pyramid' slowly increase the dose or frequency of steroid misuse, attaining a peak amount and then gradually taper off to zero, while others prefer to 'plateau', a pattern that involves alternating, overlapping, or substituting with another steroid to avoid developing a tolerance to the initial steroid (Davis, 2018; National Institute on Drug Abuse, 2018d).

Physiological Effects

"Anabolic steroids act at androgen receptors [located in muscles and tissues throughout the body to] influence cellular functioning and gene expression" (National Institute on Drug Abuse, 2018d, p. 22). The activation of these receptors regulates male characteristic development and causes a precipitous increase of calcium in the heart, brain and skeletal muscle (National Institute on Drug Abuse, 2018d).

Anabolic steroids affect the limbic system within the brain and do not have the same short-term effects on the brain as other drugs, such as activation of the reward system of the brain or the rapid increase of dopamine. While there are benefits to a controlled use of steroids, such as enhanced recovery from workouts, muscle endurance, and decrease in body fat, misuse does cause short- and long-term physical and mental effects, some of which are reversible once the drug is stopped, while others may be semi-permanent or permanent (National Institute on Drug Abuse, 2018d).

The mental effects of steroids may include feelings of well-being but also of aggression and jealousy, delusions and impaired judgment, depression and anxiety, as well as body dysmorphic disorder, while the physical effect may appear as acne/oily skin/water retention, kidney failure/liver damage, enlarged heart or stroke, just to name a few (Davis, 2018; National Institute on Drug Abuse, 2018d). There are also specific effects for men to include shrinking testicles and sperm count, baldness, and prostate and testicular cancer, while women may suffer from facial hair, cessation of menstruation, enlarged clitoris, and deepened voice (National Institute on Drug Abuse, 2018d; Preiato, 2019). Teens must also be wary as the effects last a lifetime and may include stunted height and affect overall growth (National Institute on Drug Abuse, 2018d).

Addiction/Withdrawal/Overdose

Approximately 32% of individuals who misuse steroids become dependent on them. It is not the inability of the drug to cause the same high as other drugs; rather, it is the fear of losing what has been gained that perpetuates the need (National Institute on Drug Abuse, 2018d). As a result, individuals may experience withdrawal symptoms such as fatigue, loss of appetite, mood swings, depression and even suicide as well as many other issues (National Institute on Drug Abuse, 2018d). Although rare, steroid misuse can lead to overdose and death from heart attacks, strokes, HIV, depression, suicide, and cancer (National Institute on Drug Abuse for Teens, 2020c).

Final Thoughts

Although smoking has led to over 480,000 deaths in our country per year, approximately 16.7% of adult men and 13.6% of adult women continue to smoke (Centers for Disease Control and Prevention, 2019b). Millions of individuals are living with diseases that have been acquired due to some form of drug use/abuse and addiction and 16 million individuals in the United States alone are currently living with a disease caused by smoking. (Centers for Disease Control and Prevention, 2019b).

Although the prevalence of drug use and misuse varies by age, gender, and other factors such as ease of access, individuals with mental disorders, including substance use disorders, individuals living below the poverty line, and those with low educational attainment are more likely to use and abuse drugs, such as nicotine, while youth and older adults are at particular risk for using and abusing prescription drugs (Centers for Disease Control and Prevention, 2019b).

Studies have confirmed that youth who misuse prescription medications are more likely to use other drugs such as opioids, marijuana and cocaine, smoke, and go through bouts of heavy episodic drinking (National Institute on Alcohol Abuse and Alcoholism, 2019a; National Institute on Drug Abuse, 2018a). At the other end of the age spectrum, more than 80% of individuals ages 57 to 85 use at least one prescription medication on a daily basis and more than 50% of this population takes more than five medications or supplements daily, potentially leading to the unintentional result of using a prescription medication in a way other than prescribed or intentional nonmedical use (National Institute on Drug Abuse, 2018b). Approximately 16 million individuals in the United States used prescription stimulants in 2016 and 5 million individuals misused their prescription stimulants at least once (National Institute on Drug Abuse, 2018b).

Research also demonstrated that males who have poor self-esteem, higher rates of depression, more suicide attempts, poor knowledge and attitudes about health, greater participation in sports emphasizing weight and shape, greater parental concern about weight, and higher rates of eating disorders and substance use are more likely to abuse steroids (National Institute on Drug Abuse, 2018a; National Institute on Drug Abuse, 2014a).

Points to Remember

- *There are more than one billion tobacco smokers worldwide and research shows that smoking is the most common preventable cause of death in the United States.*

- *More individuals die as a result of smoking than all deaths due to HIV, motor vehicle accidents, murder, suicide, alcohol abuse, and drug abuse combined.*

- *Nicotine, in the form of smoking tobacco, is as difficult to quit as heroin and has been found to make cocaine more addictive.*

- *Approximately 80% of individuals addicted to heroin first started with prescription opioids.*

- *Although anabolic steroids are non-addictive, those who misuse are afraid to stop due to potential loss of perceived positive changes in body composition.*

Chapter 4

Hallucinogens, Inhalants
and Other Illegal Drugs

Hallucinogens

Hallucinogens encompass a wide range of drugs that alter an individual's thoughts, perceptions, feelings, and awareness of their surroundings in a manner that can lead to significant distortions of reality (Hatfield, 2019; National Institute on Drug Abuse, 2019). Most hallucinogens are not used for medical purposes and "have a high potential for abuse and physical or psychological dependence" (Hatfield, 2019, n.p.). Hallucinogens have been used for religious purposes and/or to find enlightenment as well as for recreational and stress-relief, although there is no clear data to prove these things happen when on the high. It is estimated that approximately 1.2 million individuals over the age of 12 tried this class of drugs in 2014 (Hatfield, 2019).

Classic Hallucinogens

Classic hallucinogens are responsible for producing both auditory and visual hallucinations that cause a heightened sensory experience and/or an altered state of time and place (Hatfield, 2019; National Institute on Drug Abuse, 2019f). The effects of this drug class can begin in as little as 20 minutes once ingested and last up to 12 hours and leaves users with an altered reality that produces severe anxiety and depression (National Institute on Drug Abuse, 2014b). Four such hallucinogens include LSD, psilocybin, peyote, and DMT.

LSD (Acid, Blotter Acid, Dots, Mellow Yellow)

This drug is made from lysergic acid, found on the fungus that grows on grains such as rye (Hatfield, 2019). It is usually white or clear and odorless. LSD is one of the most dangerous hallucinogenic drugs and is known for being unpredictable, leaving users hearing sounds, seeing images, and feeling sensations that seem real, yet they do not exist (Hatfield, 2019; National Institute on Drug Abuse, 2019; National Institute on Drug Abuse, 2014b). Other effects of LSD use include but are not limited to dizziness, distorted thinking, mood swings, numbness, and loss of appetite (Hatfield, 2019; National Institute on Drug Abuse, 2014b).

Psilocybin (Little Smoke, Magic Mushrooms, Shrooms)

This substance is derived from specific types of mushrooms that can be found in the tropical and subtropical regions of Mexico, South America and the United States (Hatfield, 2019; National Institute on Drug Abuse, 2019f). According to the National Institute on Drug Abuse (2014b, 2019f), some of the effects of consuming psilocybin include feelings of relaxation, nausea/vomiting, and poisoning.

Peyote (Buttons, Cactus, Mesc)

This drug is derived from the small protrusions, or buttons, of a small, spineless cactus containing mescaline as its main ingredient. Individuals can eat the buttons or soak them in water, grind them and put them in a capsule or smoke them with tobacco or marijuana (Hatfield, 2019; National Institute on Drug Abuse, 2019f). Some of the side effects of peyote include but are not limited to vomiting, anxiety, skin flushing, issues with coordination and increased body temperature and heart rate (Hatfield, 2019).

DMT (DMT, Dimitri)

This drug is a powerful chemical found naturally in certain Amazonian plants that can be made into a hallucinogenic tea or smoked when in its synthetic crystalline form (Hatfield, 2019; National Institute on Drug Abuse, 2019f). DMT produces an intense but short-lived intoxication with effects that include but are not limited to agitation, vomiting, higher than normal heart rate and blood pressure, and distortions in body and spatial awareness (Hatfield, 2019).

Physiological Effects

Research shows that classic hallucinogens temporarily disrupt communication between brain chemical systems throughout the brain and spinal cord and interfere with the action of serotonin, which regulates mood, sensory perception, sleep, hunger, body temperature, sexual behavior, and intestinal muscle control (National Institute on Drug Abuse, 2019f).

Short-Term Effects

Classic hallucinogens can cause individuals to see images, hear sounds, and feel sensations that seem real but do not exist within 20 to 90 minutes of use and can last between 15 minutes and 12 hours (National Institute on Drug Abuse, 2019f). Although short-term effects were mentioned for individual drugs, overarching short-term effects include sleep disturbances, awkward and clumsy body movements, bizarre behaviors, psychosis and panic (National Institute on Drug Abuse, 2019f).

Long-Term Effects

There are two long-term effects that abusers of hallucinogenic drugs may experience. Persistent psychosis exists when the drug abuser suffers from continued episodes that include mood changes, paranoia, disorganized thinking and visual disturbances (National Institute on Drug Abuse, 2019f). Hallucinogen Persisting Perception Disorder (HPDD) can occur after a few days of drug use and reoccur for more than a year post abuse. It is described as "recurrences of certain drug experiences, such as hallucinations or other visual disturbances" (National Institute on Drug Abuse, 2019f). These often mimic the symptoms of brain tumors or strokes.

Dissociative Hallucinogens

Dissociative drugs cause hallucinations as well as produce feelings of detachment, such as derealization and depersonalization (Hatfield, 2019; National Institute on Drug Abuse, 2019f). Two of the most common examples of dissociative drugs are PCP and Ketamine.

PCP (Angel Dust, Peace Pill, Hog)

Originally used for a general anesthetic for surgery, it was discontinued due to its serious side effects (National Institute on Drug Abuse, 2019f). In its purest form, PCP is white and crystalline in appearance and is commonly taken orally in tablet or capsule form, smoked, snorted as a powder, or injected (Hatfield, 2019, National Institute on Drug Abuse, 2019f). The effects of PCP can vary with dosage; however, an injection or smoking produces the fastest effect within five minutes and an oral or snorted dose produces an effect within 30 minutes (Hatfield, 2019). Intoxication from PCP can last approximately 4-6 hours and short-term side effects include but are not limited to euphoria, severe anxiety, paranoia and amnesia, while long-term effects include heart attacks, brain hemorrhage, seizures or coma just to name a few (Hatfield, 2019).

Ketamine (Special K, Kit Kat)

Ketamine originated as an anesthetic for humans and animals give prior to surgery; however, most recently, it has been added to drinks as a date-rape drug (National Institute on Druse Abuse, 2019f). It is most often a white powder or clear liquid that can be mixed in liquids, injected, snorted, or smoked (Hatfield, 2019). There is a long list of side effects from ketamine use/abuse; however, a few of them are numbness, disorientation, nausea, psychosis, and delirium (Hatfield, 2019).

Physiological Effects

Dissociative hallucinogens interfere with the action of the brain chemical glutamate, which regulates pain perception, responses to the environment, emotion, and learning and memory (National Institute on Drug Abuse, 2014b). Short-term effects can appear within a few minutes of use and can last from several hours to days. In low and moderate doses, dissociative drugs can cause numbness, disorientation and loss of coordination, hallucinations, and an increase in blood pressure, heart rate, and body temperature, while in higher doses the effects include all of the previously stated issues and memory loss, physical and respiratory distress (National Institute on Drug Abuse, 2014b).

Long-Term Effects

Long-term effects may continue for a year or more after use stops and include speech problems, memory loss, weight loss, anxiety, and depression and suicidal thoughts (National Institute on Drug Abuse, 2019f). Although more research is needed into the long-term effects of dissociative drugs, current research does show that the continued use of PCP can lead to addiction, seizures, coma, and death (National Institute on Drug Abuse, 2019f).

Overdose

An overdose from drug use typically occurs when enough of a drug is consumed to produce serious adverse effects, life-threatening symptoms, or death (National Institute on Drug Abuse, 2019f). Although classic hallucinogens produce extremely unpleasant effects at high doses, those effects are not always life-threatening. Overdose is more likely with some of the dissociative drugs, such as PCP, particularly when it is taken with depressants such as alcohol or benzodiazepines (National Institute on Drug Abuse, 2019f).

Combining both classic hallucinogens and dissociative drugs pose the risk of serious harm due to the profound alteration of perception and the moods caused by drugs cause; for example, users might do things they would never do in real life or may experience and act upon profound suicidal feeling (National Institute on Drug Abuse, 2019f).

Inhalants

Inhalants contain dangerous substances that have psychoactive properties (National Institute on Drug Abuse, 2017a). Individuals inhale these substances by nose or mouth for the sole purpose of getting high, although that is not usually what they are supposed to be used for. Examples of inhalants include solvents (i.e., paint thinner, gasoline, glue), aerosol sprays (i.e., spray paint, vegetable oil spray), gases (propane tank, whipped cream aerosols), and nitrites (room deodorizer, leather cleaner) (National Institute on Drug Abuse for Teens, 2019c).

Physiological Effects

Inhalants change the make-up of the central nervous system and slow down brain activity (National Institute on Drug Abuse, 2017a). Short-term effects include slurred/distorted speech, feelings of euphoria, dizziness, and a lack of control of the body, while long-term effects may include damage to major organs of the body, vision/hearing loss, brain damage, blackouts/coma, seizures, and death (National Institute on Drug Abuse, 2017a; National Institute on Drug Abuse for Teens, 2019c).

Signs of Inhalant Use

There are many specific signs that indicate an individual has been using or abusing inhalants. Visual signs may include odors/stains on clothing, face or hands; empty/hidden containers, and odorous rags with chemicals soaked into them, while witnesses may notice that individuals under the influence experience slurred speech, loss of appetite, lack of coordination, and confusion just to name a few (National Institute on Drug Abuse, 2017a; National Institute on Drug Abuse for Teens, 2019c).

Addiction, Withdrawal and Overdose

Although uncommon, addiction to inhalants can occur when used repeatedly over a long period of time. As such, mild withdrawal symptoms can occur when the use of inhalants is stopped and can include upset stomach, loss of appetite, sweating, problems sleeping, and mood changes (National Institute on Drug Abuse for Teens, 2019c).

Inhalants, such as aerosol sprays and solvents, are highly concentrated and sniffing them may cause sudden death, where the heart stops within minutes. Seizures, coma, and death can all occur with first-time use and using inhalants with a paper or plastic bag or in an enclosed area increases the risk of death from suffocation (National Institute on Drug Abuse, 2017a).

MDMA

Typically known as Ecstasy or Molly, 3,4-methylenedioxymethamphetamine (MDMA) is a drug that alters mood and perception (National Institute on Drug Abuse, 2017b). It is similar in chemical formation to both hallucinogens and stimulants; therefore, it triggers feelings of increased emotional warmth, energy, and pleasure, while also distorting time and sensory perceptions (National Institute on Drug Abuse, 2017b).

Physiological Effects

MDMA produces both stimulant and mind-altering effects. It is toxic to nerve cells and can increase bodily functions such as blood pressure, heart rate, temperature, and heart-wall stress (National Institute on Drug Abuse, 2017b; Tackett, 2019). MDMA also increases the activity of dopamine, norepinephrine and serotonin affecting the body in different ways; for example, dopamine increases energy and reinforces behaviors in the reward center of the brain (National Institute on Drug Abuse, 2017b). Norepinephrine increases blood pressure and heart rate, while mood, sleep, appetite and sexual arousal are influenced by an increase in serotonin (National Institute on Drug Abuse, 2017b).

The list of side effects of MDMA is long and users and abusers of MDMA will notice them for three to six hours. Tackett (2019) and the National Institute on Drug Abuse (2017b) list the following as common side effects of MDMA:

- Nausea/decreased appetite/dehydration
- muscle cramping/involuntary teeth clenching
- blurred vision
- chills/sweating
- elevated blood pressure/body temperature
- vertigo/tremors/fainting
- hallucinations
- irritability/impulsiveness/aggression
- depression/anxiety/paranoia
- sleep difficulties
- memory/attention problems
- sexual dysfunction
- increased risk of hepatitis or HIV/AIDS
- liver/kidney/heart failure
- death/swelling of the brain

Addiction, Withdrawal and Overdose

Research is mixed on whether MDMA is addictive although studies have "shown that animals will self-administer doses of MDMA - an important indicator of a drug's addictive potential" (National Institute on Drug Abuse, 2017b, p. 23). Some individuals have reported addiction and withdrawal symptoms similar to those listed above (National Institute on Drug Abuse, 2017b; Tackett, 2019).

Fatal overdoses of MDMA are rare but the use of MDMA can cause a number of acute adverse health effects that are potentially life threatening. Of most concern is the ability of MDMA to affect the body's ability to control temperature. When used in active, hot environments, MDMA can cause hyperthermia, leading to swelling of the brain, kidney, liver, or heart failure, and death (National Institute on Drug Abuse, 2017b).

Heroin

A psychoactive natural substance, heroin, is made from morphine and can be found in the resin of the seed pod of opium poppy plants (National Institute on Drug Abuse, 2019d). It is a white or brown powder, or a black sticky substance known as black tar heroin (National Institute on Drug Abuse, 2018g). Powdered heroin can be mixed with water and injected directly into an individual's vein or it can be sniffed, smoked, snorted, or combined with other drugs, such as alcohol or cocaine (National Institute on Drug Abuse, 2018g).

Physiological Effects

Regardless of the method or point of entry, heroin enters the brain rapidly, converts to morphine and binds to and activates receptors, which then stimulate the release of dopamine thus reinforcing drug-taking behavior (National Institute on Drug Abuse, 2018g; Patterson, 2018a). This release causes a 'rush' that produces a calm/warm feeling, a heaviness in the legs and arms as well as an "increased sense of well-being and confidence" (Patterson, 2018a, n.p.).

Short- and Long-Term Effects

Heroin affects individuals differently depending on size, weight and health, the amount of the drug used, the regularity that they use the drug, if they combine it with other drugs and the strength of the heroin available (Alcohol and Drug Foundation, 2019). In addition to feelings of euphoria and pleasure, individuals may also feel effects such as bodily flushing, nausea/vomiting, confusion/drowsiness/semi-consciousness, intense pleasure/pain responses, slurred/slow speech and clouded mental functioning (Alcohol and Drug Foundation, 2019; National Institute on Drug Abuse, 2019d; National Institute on Drug Abuse, 2018g).

The list of long-term effects is substantial and includes a wide range of issues such as insomnia, damage to all bodily organs, sexual dysfunction, mental disorders, constipation/stomach cramping, collapsed or damaged veins, and financial/work/social issues (Alcohol and Drug Foundation, 2019; National Institute on Drug Abuse, 2019d; National Institute on Drug Abuse, 2018g).

Addiction, Withdrawal and Overdose

Heroin is highly addictive and in 2016 approximately 626,000 individuals in the United States had a heroin use disorder (Alcohol and Drug Foundation, 2019; National Institute on Drug Abuse, 2019d; National Institute on Drug Abuse for Teens, 2019c; Patterson, 2018a). Research has shown that repeated heroin use changes the physical structure and physiology of the brain, creates irreversible long-term imbalances in neuronal and hormonal systems, and deteriorates white matter in the brain (National Institute on Drug Abuse, 2018g). When use is stopped abruptly, individuals may have severe withdrawal symptoms starting within 6 to 24 hours, lasting up to a week, that include many of the symptoms listed above in addition to muscle/bone pain, runny nose and fast heartbeat, cold flashes and goosebumps, severe depression (National Institute on Drug Abuse 2018g; Patterson, 2018a).

Consuming a large amount of heroin can lead to overdose and death, particularly if the batch is strong, or the heroin is mixed with another unknown substance (Alcohol and Drug Foundation, 2019). Research shows that there were more than 15,000 deaths caused by heroin overdose in 2017 (Centers for Disease Control and Prevention, 2019a). Signs of overdose include extremely slow breathing/blue lips/fingertips, cold/clammy skin, vomiting/gurgling noises, uncontrollable shaking, passing out/death (Alcohol and Drug Foundation, 2019; National Institute on Drug Abuse, 2019d; Patterson, 2018a).

Final Thoughts

Hallucinogens, inhalants, MDMA, and heroin, while providing initial feelings of euphoria and well-being, have lasting negative and harmful consequences. Research shows that all of these drugs disrupt communication in an individual's brain and interfere with the action of several neurotransmitters that regulate mood, sensory perception, body temperature, sexual behavior, pain perception, environmental response, and learning and memory. Most importantly, these chemical changes reinforce drug-taking behavior, causing individuals to become addicted. In 2016 alone, approximately 170,000 individuals started using heroin, raising the total number of individuals using heroin that year to 950,000 (National Institute on Drug Abuse, 2018g). With all drugs, the risk of overdose and death is significant, even with the first use, due to concentration, unknown additives, and polydrug abuse.

Points to Remember

- *Death can occur with the first use of an inhalant, even in a young, healthy individual.*

- *Hallucinogens are used for a variety of purposes to include religious, stress-relief, recreational, or to reach a place of perceived enlightenment or understanding.*

- *Regardless of the drug, the short- and long-term effects can be gruesome and cause damage to the organs of the body as well as to the social, work and family units.*

- *Hallucinogens are highly addictive, and the withdrawal of such drugs is difficult.*

Chapter 5

Treatment for Substance Abuse Addictions

Drug addiction is a "chronic, relapsing disorder characterized by compulsive drug seeking, continued use despite harmful consequences, and long-lasting changes in the brain" (U.S. Department of Health and Human Services, 2018, p. 1). According to a 2018 national survey on drug use, 21.2 million people (7.8% of the U.S. population) aged 12 or older needed treatment for an illicit drug or alcohol use problem and only 3.7 million of these individuals (1.4%) received any substance use treatment (Substance Abuse and Mental Health Services Administration, 2019).

Long-term treatment for addiction can assist individuals in stopping using drugs, stay drug-free, and be productive within their family and place of employment, and as a member of society (National Institute on Drug Abuse, 2018h). Effective evidenced-based treatment programs are based on the knowledge that "addiction is a complex but treatable disease that affects brain function and behavior" (National Institute on Drug Abuse, 2018h). While no single treatment is right for every individual, quick access to treatment and the length of time spent in treatment is critical (National Institute on Drug Abuse, 2018h).

Research demonstrates that the most effective treatments address all of an individual's needs including other possible mental health disorders, not just their drug use, and that treatment plans must be reviewed and modified as needs change (National Institute on Drug Abuse, 2018h). Whether behavioral therapy or medication is used independently of one another or in combination, drug use during treatment must be continuously monitored and individuals should be tested for HIV/AIDS, hepatitis B and C, tuberculosis, and other infectious diseases as well as provided the knowledge needed to reduce their risk of contracting an infectious disease (National Institute on Drug Abuse, 2018h).

Evidenced-Based Treatment Models and Approaches

The best treatment for addiction begins with prevention (National Institute on Drug Abuse 2019g). Regardless of the approach, prevention models focus on helping afflicted individuals develop the attitudes, knowledge and skills necessary to change negative behaviors and make appropriate choices

(Substance Abuse and Mental Health Services Administration, 2019). There are a wide range of evidence-based treatment programs that can be used in family systems, schools, and communities that are known to positively alter the balance between risk and protective factors associated with drug use by increasing a person's protective factors while eliminating or reducing their risk factors (National Institute on Drug Abuse, 2019g; Substance Abuse and Mental Health Services Administration, 2019).

Universal programs address risk and protective factors common to all children in a particular setting, such as a school or community while selective programs target groups of children and teens who have increased risk factors for drug use (National Institute on Drug Abuse, 2018h; National Institute on Drug Abuse, 2014a). Indicated programs are available for youth who have already started using drugs (National Institute on Drug Abuse, 2018h; National Institute on Drug Abuse, 2014a). Research has shown that drug use trends are affected by cultural and social factors and when drug use is perceived harmful by today's youth, the level of use is reduced (National Institute on Drug Abuse, 2014a).

Medications and Medical Devices

Certain treatment medications can help the brain gradually adapt to the absence of the abused drug by slowly staving off drug cravings and creating a calming effect on the body's systems, enabling a person to focus on related drug treatment such as counseling and other psychotherapies (National Institute on Drug Abuse, 2014a). Depending on the stage of treatment, different medications may be prescribed to assist an individual in refraining from drug use, remain in a treatment program and/or avoid falling back into bad habits (National Institute on Drug Abuse, 2014a).

Withdrawal & Detoxification

Numerous physical and emotional symptoms, including depression, anxiety, and other mood disorders, as well as restlessness and/or sleeplessness can occur with the cessation of drug use. Specific medications are designed to suppress, treat, and reduce these symptoms, making it easier for a person to stop the drug use (National Institute on Drug Abuse, 2014a). Research shows that such medications have been used in almost 80% of detoxifications occurring in treatment facilities (National Institute on Drug Abuse, 2019g). Medications are currently available for the treatment of opioid, nicotine, and alcohol addiction, while medications to treat stimulant and marijuana addiction are still being developed (National Institute on Drug Abuse, 2019g).

Opioids

In 2017, the Food and Drug Administration (FDA, 2017) approved an electronic stimulation device that helps in reducing opioid withdrawal symptoms. When placed behind the ear, it sends electrical impulses to "stimulate branches of certain cranial nerves" (FDA, 2017, n.p.). In 2018, lofexidine hydrochloride was approved as a non-opioid medication designed to reduce opioid withdrawal symptoms (FDA, 2018).

Methadone, buprenorphine, and Naltrexone® are also used to treat opioid addiction and affect the brain in the same way as heroin and morphine (National Institute on Drug Abuse, 2018h). While methadone and buprenorphine suppress withdrawal symptoms and relieve cravings, Naltrexone® blocks the effects of opioids at the brain's receptor site (called an antagonist) and can only be used with individuals who have gone through detoxification (National Institute on Drug Abuse, 2019g; National Institute on Drug Abuse, 2018i).

Methadone. Methadone is a long-acting mu-opioid receptor full antagonist that reduces opioid cravings and withdrawal by blunting or blocking the effects of illicit opioids (National Institute on Drug Abuse, 2018i; Substance Abuse and Mental Health Services Administration, 2019). Methadone must be given under the supervision of a physician, with treatment lasting a minimum of 12 months (Substance Abuse and Mental Health Services Administration, 2019).

Buprenorphine. Produced in either a pure form taken sublingually or in combination with naloxone to form Suboxone®, this drug is a synthetic opioid medication that "acts as a partial agonist at opioid receptors - it does not produce the euphoria and sedation caused by heroin or other opioids" (National Institute on Drug Abuse, 2018h, p. 40). When Suboxone is taken as prescribed, naloxone has no effect; however, if Suboxone® is injected by an individual who is addicted, "naloxone will produce severe withdrawal effects… [that lessen] the likelihood that the drug will be abused" (National Institute on Drug Abuse, 2018h, p. 41).

Naltrexone®. Naltrexone® is a non-addictive "synthetic opioid antagonist [that] blocks opioids from binding to their receptors and thereby prevents their euphoric and other effects" (National Institute on Drug Abuse, 2018h, p. 42). It is routinely used to treat opioid addiction and in the reversal of opioid overdose (National Institute on Drug Abuse, 2018h). To prevent withdrawal, Naltrexone® should be administered in residential settings; however, it is more commonly prescribed in outpatient settings, resulting in high numbers of non-compliant individuals. As such, Naltrexone® is best suited for recently detoxified individuals who are highly motivated to attain total abstinence due to external circumstances (i.e., professional, parolees) (National Institute on Drug Abuse, 2018h).

Naloxone. Naloxone is an opioid antagonist that rapidly reverses opioid overdoses by blocking opioid receptor sites and reversing the toxic effects of an overdose drug (Schiller & Mechanic, 2019). Individuals who would benefit from naloxone include those:

- *taking high doses of opioids for long-term management of chronic pain;*
- *receiving rotating opioid medication regimens (and so are at risk for incomplete cross-tolerance);*
- *discharged from emergency medical care following opioid poisoning or poisoning;*
- *taking certain /long-acting preparations that may increase risk for opioid overdose.*

(Anderson, 2014, n.p.)

Nicotine

Nicotine replacement therapies (NRT) include over the counter products such as the patch, spray, gum, and lozenges. The FDA has also approved two prescription medications, bupropion and varenicline, to assist in the prevention of relapse in individuals trying to quit (Rigotti, 2020). In order to reduce cravings, withdrawal symptoms and possible relapse, NRT stimulates the brain receptors that are influenced by nicotine (National Institute on Drug Abuse, 2020). Research demonstrates that replacement therapies increase the rate at which individuals quit smoking by 50-70% and that the most effective cessation strategy is one in which there is both a continual nicotine delivery through a transdermal patch and another form of nicotine such as gum, inhaler, lozenges, or spray (National Institute on Drug Abuse, 2020).

Bupropion. Bupropion was originally approved as an antidepressant but was found to lessen the urge to smoke in individuals with depression and is now used for individuals who wish to stop smoking that do not have a co-occurring mental illness (National Institute on Drug Abuse, 2020). Bupropion both inhibits the reuptake and stimulates the release of norepinephrine and dopamine in the brain and short- and long-term studies have shown it to be as effective as nicotine replacement therapies for smoking cessation (National Institute on Drug Abuse, 2019h).

Varenicline. Varenicline reduces nicotine cravings by stimulating nicotinic receptors in the brain and has been found to be more effective than any single form of NRT (National Institute on Drug Abuse, 2020). Research has found that individuals on varenicline, either alone or combined with therapy, were more likely to remain abstinent from smoking (Bullen et al., 2018).

Alcohol

There are several medications that have been approved by the FDA to treat alcohol addiction. Naltrexone® suppresses the euphoria associated with alcohol and reduces relapse to heavy drinking in the same way it does for opioid abuse (National Institute on Drug Abuse, 2018h). For severe addiction, Acamprosate® reduces withdrawal symptoms such as anxiety, dysphoria, insomnia, and restlessness (National Institute on Drug Abuse, 2018h). Individuals who are highly motivated to stop drinking can take Disulfiram®, a drug that negates the breakdown of alcohol and increases the build-up of acetaldehyde (National Institute on Drug Abuse, 2018h). With higher levels of acetaldehyde come more severe reactions such as irregular heartbeat, nausea and flushing of the body and face when alcohol is consumed (National Institute on Drug Abuse, 2018h).

Naltrexone®. In individuals suffering from alcohol use disorder, Naltrexone® does not reduce the craving for alcohol or reduce the symptoms of alcohol withdrawal; rather, it suppresses the euphoria and pleasurable sensations that come from drinking alcohol, making individuals less likely to consume (Juergens 2019a).

Particularly useful for those individuals that have relapsed, Naltrexone® is most effective when taken in conjunction with other forms of treatment, such as counseling and community-based recovery groups (Juergens, 2019a). Although the effectiveness of this medication is limited and can be dangerous for individuals with alcohol-related liver damage, Naltrexone® has fewer and less severe side effects than other treatments and its therapeutic benefits outweigh any potential side effect that does occur (Juergens, 2019a).

Acamprosate®. Acamprosate®, one of the most common medications prescribed for alcohol abuse treatment, it reduces the brain's dependence on alcohol by impacting glutamate and gamma-aminobutyric acid neurotransmitter systems to modulate and normalize the chaotic brain activity that occurs with the sudden cessation of alcohol consumption (Juergens, 2019c; National Institute on Drug Abuse, 2018h). While Acamprosate® does not reduce the euphoria associated with alcohol or create deterring side effects from alcohol use, it can reduce symptoms of protracted withdrawal such as anxiety, dysphoria, insomnia and restlessness (Juergens, 2019c; National Institute on Drug Abuse, 2018h).

One of the advantages of Acamprosate® is that it is broken down by the digestive tract, not the liver, and can be used by individuals who suffer from alcohol-associated liver-related health concerns (Juergens, 2019c). This medication should only be used after individuals have ceased all alcohol use and under initial detoxification and works best when combined with therapy and other medications such as Naltrexone® and Disulfiram® (Juergens, 2019c). Research has shown that the use of Acamprosate® is more effective in individuals with severe dependence and has assisted in maintaining abstinence for several weeks up to several months in those afflicted by dependence (National Institute on Drug Abuse, 2018h).

Disulfiram®. Disulfiram® interferes with the body's digestion, absorption, and degradation of alcohol and when an individual drinks while taking Disulfiram®, the accumulation of acetaldehyde occurs, producing similar effects to those of Naltrexone® (Juergens, 2019b).

Research demonstrates that cravings for alcohol are not reduced by Disulfiram® yet its effects on the body serve as an effective deterrent and enable individuals to remain sober (Juergens, 2019b). This Disulfiram®-ethanol reaction can be severe, and in some cases fatal; therefore, it should only be taken by individuals who have gone through withdrawal and detoxification, have abstained from alcohol for a minimum of 12 hours, and have a blood alcohol level of zero (Juergens, 2019b). Although compliance with the drug can be poor, those individuals who are highly motivated find it to be effective, particularly for those who use Disulfiram® to manage high-risk situations (National Institute on Drug Abuse, 2018h).

Research indicates that Disulfiram® is most effective when taken in conjunction with other medications such as Acamprosate®; however, it is not sufficient to treat alcoholism unless incorporated into a larger treatment regimen that includes rehabilitation, therapy, counseling, and/or 12-step programs (Juergens, 2019b).

Outpatient Behavioral Therapies

Research shows that combining treatment medications with behavioral therapy is the most successful way to ensure success for the majority of addicts and that treatment approaches must be tailored to address each individual's drug use patterns and drug-related medical, psychiatric, and social problems (National Institute on Drug Abuse, 2014a).

Behavioral treatments can modify an individual's attitude and behavior toward drug use and increase their life skills and interrelated ability to handle stressful situations and environmental cues that may trigger intense cravings for drugs. Engaging in behavioral therapy can also enhance the effectiveness of medications and help individuals remain in treatment longer (National Institute on Drug Abuse 2019g; National Institute on Drug Abuse, 2014a).

Drug use often interferes with an individual's physical health and disrupts their ability to function as part of the family, at work, and in the community and, as such, treatment must address the needs of the whole individual to be successful (National Institute on Drug Abuse, 2014a).

Cognitive Behavioral Therapy

Cognitive Behavioral Therapy (CBT) is a present-oriented, problem-focused, and goal-directed active therapeutic modality that explores individual patterns of behavior that may lead to self-destructive actions and beliefs and seeks to help individuals recognize, avoid, and cope with the circumstances and situations in which they are most likely to abuse drugs (American Addiction Centers, 2019a; Juergens, 2019d).

This therapy seeks to find connections between thoughts, feelings, and actions and to increase awareness of how these impact recovery (Juergens 2019d; National Institute on Drug Abuse, 2014a). In addition to addiction, CBT treats co-occurring disorders such as anxiety, attention deficit disorder, bipolar disorder, obsessive compulsive disorder, eating disorders, and post-traumatic distress disorder (Juergens, 2019d).

Through CBT, addicted individuals learn that a multitude of harmful actions and emotions are not logical or rational and may arise from past experiences or environmental factors (Juergens, 2019d). When certain feelings and actions are understood, as well as how those feelings and actions led to substance abuse and addiction, individuals with addiction are better able to overcome their addiction (Juergens, 2019d).

CBT Techniques

Using specific CBT techniques to explore the positive and negative consequences of substance use, addicted individuals can learn to manage their triggers by recognizing and identifying the circumstances that led to their substance use, avoiding and removing themselves from any triggering situations, and using learned CBT techniques to address and alleviate the emotions and thoughts that may have led to their substance use (American Addiction Centers, 2019a; Juergens, 2019d).

Behavioral Experiments. Some individuals respond better to positive and kind thoughts, while others respond better to soft criticism. Using behavioral experiments, individuals try both to see which works better to change their behavior (Addiction Center, n.d.).

Imagery Based Exposure. By remembering painful or negative memories and paying attention to the emotion, impulse, sight, sound and thought, recovering addicts can replace those memories with more positive behaviors that negate the need for drugs or alcohol (Hales et al., 2015).

Pleasant Activity Schedule. Breaking up the daily and weekly schedule into manageable parts using routines, the activity schedule produces positive thinking and supports the growth of healthy habits (Addiction Center, n.d.).

Thought Records. An examination of thought patterns is used to find "objective evidence supporting or disproving" (Addiction Center, n.d., n.p.) the reason for these negative thoughts. The individual produces a list of pros and cons regarding said evidence and uses the list to compare and contrast (Addiction Center, n.d.). This critical evaluation will assist addicted individuals to attain more balanced thinking and dismiss any false beliefs and insecurities that may have led to their substance abuse (Addiction Center, n.d.).

Contingency Management. Contingency Management uses operant conditioning and behaviorism to increase positive behaviors, while decreasing or eliminating negative behaviors (Patterson, 2017). Contingency management treatment for addiction involves the use of positive reinforcement (i.e. rewards or privileges) for not only remaining drug free, but for attending and participating in counseling sessions, and/or for taking treatment medications as prescribed (Patterson, 2017).

Voucher-Based Reinforcement. Providing vouchers for drug-free living through urine tests, the vouchers begin with low monetary incentives and become more lucrative as urine tests continue to be negative (National Institute on Drug Abuse, 2018h). A positive urine test brings the voucher back to a beginning amount. Vouchers can be used for items such as food, movie passes, or other goods or services that are consistent with a drug-free lifestyle (Patterson, 2017).

Prize Incentive. Similar in structure to VBR, the prize incentives are given as a way to possibly win items, although there is no guarantee. Over the course of a minimum 3-month program that meets one or more times per week, individuals who supply drug-free urine samples, attend counseling sessions and complete weekly goal-oriented activities, or take medications as prescribed draw from a container for the chance to win a prize worth between $1 and $100 (National Institute on Drug Abuse, 2018h; Patterson, 2017).

Community Reinforcement Approach Plus Vouchers

This intensive 24-week outpatient therapy is for individuals addicted to alcohol and cocaine. It uses a range of reinforcements (i.e. family, recreational, social) coupled with material incentives to create a lifestyle that those addicted to drugs or alcohol will find more rewarding than the life of substance abuse (National Institute on Drug Abuse, 2018h). Treatment goals include learning life skills in a manner that sustains abstinence and reducing the consumption of alcohol for those who mix the liquid with cocaine (National Institute on Drug Abuse 2018h).

During treatment, individuals attend one or two weekly individual counseling sessions to improve family relations, learn a multitude of skills to minimize the need for drugs, and develop new interests and social networks (National Institute on Drug Abuse, 2018h). Similar to Voucher-Based Reinforcement, urine samples are submitted two or three times a week and individuals receive vouchers for clean samples (National Institute on Drug Abuse, 2018h).

Family Therapy

Family Therapy refers to a group of treatment styles that targets the family rather than the affected individual and the dynamics that could be contributing to their drug use (Patterson, 2018b; National Institute on Drug Abuse, 2014a). The underlying belief of family therapy is that families share a connection; therefore, changing one component, changes all components and the unwanted behaviors can be eradicated (Patterson, 2018b).

This integrated approach emphasizes the strengths of the complete family and that the family's health plays a significant role in the success of an individual's recovery while substance use can be eliminated for the family unit (Patterson, 2018b). Through therapy, families are engaged in specific strategies that focus on developing problem-solving skills, give each family member a sense of accountability and a reason to change (Patterson, 2018b).

In addition to the addicted family member gaining an awareness of their needs and behaviors, the entire family will learn and understand the systems in place that support and deter substance abuse, including any codependent behavior that is preventing recovery, and understand and avoid enabling behaviors (Patterson, 2018b). As a result, the mental and physical state of the family system, communication styles, and relationship quality will improve (Patterson, 2018b).

It is important to note that family therapy can be completed in combination with other treatment modalities such as individual therapy, group therapy, medication management, and residential rehabilitation programs (Patterson, 2018b).

Family Behavior Therapy. Family Behavior Therapy combines behavioral contracting with contingency management to target the substance use as well as any co-occurring mental health issues, defiance, family problems, employment, and financial concerns (National Institute on Drug Abuse, 2018h; Patterson, 2018b). In therapy, individuals are encouraged to develop behavioral goals for preventing substance abuse while families are encouraged to use learned behavioral strategies to improve the home environment with rewards being provided by significant others for reaching set goals (National Institute on Drug Abuse, 2018h).

Multidimensional Family Therapy. Multidimensional Family Therapy is used with adolescents that have drug abuse problems as well as their families to address a range of influences on drug abuse patterns and to improve overall family functioning (Patterson, 2018b). Family sessions explore ways to positively impact their children and curb substance use as well as parenting styles, while individual sessions give adolescents the strategies needed to make decisions, communicate and problem solve in meaningful and acceptable ways (Patterson, 2018b).

Motivational Enhancement Therapy. Motivational Enhancement Therapy facilitates treatment entry and aims to stop drug use by using strategies that "evoke rapid and internally motivated change" (National Institute on Drug Abuse, 2018h, p. 55). An initial assessment battery session is conducted followed by two to four individual treatment sessions in which personal substance use and coping strategies are discussed and self-motivational statements are elicited by the therapist to strengthen an individual's motivation and create a plan for change (National Institute on Drug Abuse, 2018h). Subsequent sessions monitor the change in the individual, encourage individuals to strengthen their commitment to change or abstinence and review strategies to help them cope with the changes that are occurring (National Institute on Drug Abuse, 2018h).

Research indicates that Motivational Enhancement Therapy is most effective with individuals addicted to alcohol and marijuana while results are mixed for individuals who abuse other drugs such as heroin, cocaine, and/or nicotine (National Institute on Drug Abuse, 2018h).

Motivational Interviewing

Motivational interviewing uses psychotherapy to choose more positive outcomes instead of the negative ones previously preferred (Patterson, 2018c). The therapist's role in this situation is one of support, thus allowing the individual the ability to make their own choices and arrive at their own conclusions without feeling any pressure to do so (Patterson, 2018c).

During motivational interviewing, the therapist attempts to view a situation from the addicted individual's point of view, draws out individual perceptions, and assists the individual in creating an internal desire for change, thus giving the addicted individual a sense of empowerment to become autonomous in their decision-making ability (Patterson, 2018c).

Matrix Model

This framework helps those who have abused stimulants understand how treatment can change the course of their lives through abstinence. Abusers are informed about addiction and possible relapse as well as how to make the necessary changes, receive support and find appropriate self-help programs (National Institute on Drug Abuse, 2018h; Patterson, 2018d). Treatment materials include "elements of relapse prevention, family and group therapies, drug education, and self-help participation [as well as] family education groups, early recovery skills groups, relapse prevention groups, combined sessions, urine tests, 12-step programs, relapse analysis, and social support groups" (National Institute on Drug Abuse, 2018h, p. 57).

In this model, the therapist serves as both teacher and coach to foster a positive, encouraging relationship with the addicted individual that reinforces positive behavior change and promotes self-esteem, dignity, and self-worth (National Institute on Drug Abuse 2018h; Patterson, 2018d). The therapist is also responsible for creating a safe, nonjudgmental environment based on positivity and openness and building an empathic understanding with addicted individuals and promote their needs (Patterson, 2018d).

The Matrix Model incorporates techniques from CBT while using motivational interviewing skills to reduce an individual's ambivalence (National Institute on Drug Abuse 2018h). Family members may be included in sessions to address the individual's current needs and educate the family on issues associated with substance abuse, addiction, and dependence (National Institute on Drug Abuse, 2018h).

Relapse prevention groups are also used to educate individuals in identifying the signs of relapse early so it can be prevented and include topics such as shame, guilt, and resentment, appropriate uses of time, building motivation, identification of relapse triggers, building self-monitoring skills, and downplaying the role of willpower (National Institute on Drug Abuse, 2018h).

Research indicates that working with a therapist that uses the Matrix Model, individuals demonstrate "statistically significant reductions in drug and alcohol use, improvements in psychological indicators, and reduced risky sexual behaviors associated with HIV transmission" (National Institute on Drug Abuse, 2018h, p. 57).

Community-Based Recovery Groups

12-Step Programs

Twelve-step therapies require the abuser to be an active participant in their return to health (National Institute on Drug Abuse, 2018h). A central tenet of step programs is the notion of acceptance and the "realization that drug addiction is a chronic, progressive disease over which an individual has no control, that life has become unmanageable because of drugs, that willpower alone is insufficient to overcome the problem, and that abstinence is the only alternative" (National Institute on Drug Abuse, 2018h, p. 58).

Another tenet is that of surrender, which involves following a specific list of tasks, readily accepting the fellowship of others in similar circumstances, and giving oneself over to a higher power (National Institute on Drug Abuse, 2018h, p. 58). The third tenet involves active involvement in meetings and activities that add to the program (National Institute on Drug Abuse, 2018h).

Alcoholics Anonymous

This is a "nonprofessional, self-supporting, multiracial, apolitical" (Alcoholics Anonymous World Services, Inc., 2020, n.p.) international group of more than 2 million men and women worldwide who have had issues with alcohol (Alcoholics Anonymous World Services, Inc., 2020, n.p.). The group is open to anyone who has a drinking problem and is willing to accept help regardless of educational level or participant age (Alcoholics Anonymous World Services, Inc., 2020).

In both closed and open meetings, discussion is not required but individuals are encouraged to share stories about their "journey to sobriety [while others] interject and support or share their story, or provide advice" (Juergens, 2019e, n.p.). While recovering addicts are the only individuals allowed at closed meetings, spouses, family members and friends of a recovering addict are allowed to attend open meetings (Juergens, 2019e).

The twelve steps of Alcoholics Anonymous are a "group of principles, spiritual in nature, which, if practiced as a way of life, can expel the obsession to drink alcohol and enable the sufferer to become happily and usefully whole" (Alcoholics Anonymous World Services, Inc., 2020). Although the steps are written in linear form, individuals view them as an ongoing circle and specific steps may be revisited until an individual is comfortable in that stage of the recovery process (Juergens, 2019e).

Alcoholics Anonymous World Services, Inc. (2020) lists the twelve steps as

1. *We admitted we were powerless over alcohol—that our lives had become unmanageable.*

2. *Came to believe that a Power greater than ourselves could restore us to sanity.*

3. *Made a decision to turn our will and our lives over to the care of God as we understood Him.*

4. *Made a searching and fearless moral inventory of ourselves.*

5. *Admitted to God, to ourselves, and to another human being the exact nature of our wrongs.*

6. *Were entirely ready to have God remove all these defects of character.*

7. *Humbly asked Him to remove our shortcomings.*

8. *Made a list of all persons we had harmed and became willing to make amends to them all.*

9. *Made direct amends to such people wherever possible, except when to do so would injure them or others.*

10. *Continued to take personal inventory and when we were wrong promptly admitted it.*

11. *Sought through prayer and meditation to improve our conscious contact with God as we understood Him, praying only for knowledge of His will for us and the power to carry that out.*

12. *Having had a spiritual awakening as the result of these steps, we tried to carry this message to alcoholics, and to practice these principles in all our affairs.*

(n.p.).

Unlike the Twelve Steps, the Twelve Traditions of Alcoholics Anonymous speak to how individual members behave as a group and include:

1. *Our common welfare should come first; personal recovery depends upon AA unity.*

2. *For our group purpose there is but one ultimate authority–a loving God as He may express Himself in our group conscience. Our leaders are but trusted servants; they do not govern.*

3. *The only requirement for AA membership is a desire to stop drinking.*

4. *Each group should be autonomous except in matters affecting other groups or AA as a whole.*

5. *Each group has but one primary purpose–to carry its message to the alcoholic who still suffers.*

6. *An AA group ought never endorse, finance, or lend the AA name to any related facility or outside enterprise, lest problems of money, property and prestige divert us from our primary purpose.*

7. *Every AA group ought to be fully self-supporting, declining outside contributions.*

8. *Alcoholics Anonymous should remain forever nonprofessional, but our service centers may employ special workers.*

9. *AA, as such, ought never be organized; but we may create service boards or committees directly responsible to those they serve.*

10. *Alcoholics Anonymous has no opinion on outside issues; hence the AA name ought never be drawn into public controversy.*

11. *Our public relations policy is based on attraction rather than promotion; we need always maintain personal anonymity at the level of press, radio and films.*

12. *Anonymity is the spiritual foundation of all our traditions, ever reminding us to place principles before personalities.*

(Alcoholics Anonymous World Services, Inc., 2020, n.p.).

Al-Anon

Al-Anon treats the disease of alcoholism as a family illness and as such, supports the friends and family members of individuals who have issues with drinking (Juergens, 2019f). Founded by the wife of the creator of Alcoholics Anonymous, Al-Anon is an anonymous, nonreligious-based organization that holds a variety of meetings centered on its own 12 step program that is adapted, nearly verbatim, from that of Alcoholics Anonymous (Juergens, 2019f). Meetings focus on sharing experiences, understanding they are not to blame for the alcoholism and how they can move forward as a family (Juergens, 2019f).

Narcotics Anonymous

Narcotics Anonymous (NA) is a global, community-based organization with a multi-lingual and multicultural membership that offers recovery from the effects of addiction through a twelve-step program, including regular attendance at group meetings (Narcotics Anonymous World Services, 2018). Although there are references to a higher power, or God, NA is non-denominational, and uses those references to connect individuals to a common fellowship or spirituality (Narcotics Anonymous World Services, 2018). The 12 steps of Alcoholics Anonymous are used in meetings with the only difference being that the word "alcohol" is replaced by the word "addiction" (Juergens, 2019g).

Narcotics Anonymous provides support through either open or closed meetings for individuals attempting to recover from drug addiction (Juergens, 2019g). Using a discussion format, any individual member can share personal stories of addiction and recovery as they relate to their lives and in speaker meetings, one or more specific members are asked to share their stories for the majority of the meeting (Juergens, 2019g). Members are not required to share, although for those that choose to, sharing is done one at a time and limited to a member's own experiences (Juergens, 2019g).

Inpatient and Residential Treatment

Licensed residential treatment facilities offering 24-hour intensive care is an excellent option for individuals who simply need a more structured environment or support (National Institute on Drug Abuse, 2019g). These facilities offer medical attention, housing and a plethora of therapeutic approaches to meet the needs of those in treatment (National Institute on Drug Abuse, 2019g). These programs focus on helping recovering addicts "live a drug-free, crime-free lifestyle after treatment" (National Institute on Drug Abuse, 2019g, n.p.).

Therapeutic Communities

Therapeutic communities are highly structured, recovery-oriented programs in which individuals remain in residence for 6-12 months and the entire community, including staff and recovering residents, act as key agents of change, influencing the patient's attitudes, understanding, and behaviors associated with drug use (National Institute on Drug Abuse, 2015).

Focus is given to the whole individual and overall lifestyle changes instead of just abstinence from drug use. The chronic, relapsing nature of addiction is acknowledged, and relapse is seen as an opportunity for learning use. Recovery is viewed as a "gradual, ongoing process of cognitive change through clinical interventions [that happens over time]" (National Institute on Drug Abuse, 2015, p. 2)

As a member of a drug-free therapeutic community, individuals are encouraged to examine their personal behavior and to engage in the "principles of honesty, taking responsibility, hard work, and the willingness to learn" (National Institute on Drug Abuse, 2015, p. 2). As an individual progresses through each stage of recovery, they are tasked with increased personal and social responsibility (National Institute on Drug Abuse, 2015). Within this community, those same individuals participate in "group living and activities to drive individual change and attainment of therapeutic goals" (National Institute on Drug Abuse, 2015, p. 3).

A central tenet of these communities is that "self- and mutual-help are seen as a mechanism for changing their overall lifestyle and identity" (National Institute on Drug Abuse, 2015, p. 4). The mutual-help process uses a variety of activities such as group discussion, individual counseling, community-based meetings, games and role-playing to help change negative patterns of thought and behavior and build self-efficacy (National Institute on Drug Abuse, 2015).

Members of the community are encouraged to be accountable for their behaviors, set personal well-being goals, positively participate in the broader community and life in general after leaving treatment, and ultimately, identify, express, and manage their feelings in appropriate and positive ways (National Institute on Drug Abuse, 2015).

Short-Term Residential Treatment

Short-term residential treatment focuses on detoxification and provides initial intensive counseling and preparation for treatment in a community-based setting using a modified 12-step approach (National Institute on Drug Abuse, 2018h). Residential treatments are recommended for individuals who have increased "stressors and triggers in their environment, low availability of support, a history of chronic substance abuse, and/or poor treatment outcomes in the past" (American Addiction Centers, n.d.a).

Set in home, apartment, or dormitory type environments, residential treatment programs provide a safe and drug-free environment in which individual and group therapy sessions are provided along with access to medical services, nutritional counseling, wellness activities, and planning for aftercare programs (American Addiction Centers, n.d.a).

Recovery Housing

Recovery housing, such as sober living homes, provides supervised, short-term housing for individuals following other types of inpatient or residential treatment and assists in the transition to an independent life (American Addiction Centers, 2020b). These settings provide a "supportive network for individuals who may not be ready to face the stress of everyday life and require additional time to hone the coping mechanisms, communication, and self-reliance skills taught during rehab" (American Addiction Centers, 2020b, n.p.).

Recovery housing is best matched with individuals who "suffer from medical or mental health issues in addition to problems with substance abuse and/or addiction, individuals who have been through rehab previously on one or more occasions, those without a strong support system in place at home, and individuals who may be resistant to treatment" (American Addiction Centers, 2020b, n.p.).

Final Thoughts

Drug addiction is a chronic, relapsing brain disease best dealt with by preventative measures that focus on helping individuals develop the knowledge, attitudes, and skills needed to make good choices, change harmful behaviors, stop using drugs, stay drug-free, and be a productive member of society.

Beyond prevention, there are a multitude of pharmacotherapies and behavioral treatments that can assist individuals to remain abstinent and adapt to living without substances. While medications can stave off drug cravings, they can also enable an individual to focus on related behavioral treatments such as cognitive behavioral therapy, family therapy, and contingency management, among others. Using different therapeutic modalities, individuals learn how to identify problematic actions, beliefs, thoughts, feelings, and environments that perpetuate drug use as well as engage and live in a drug-free lifestyle. To aid in this transition and provide a safe, steady source of support, community-based recovery groups help individuals regain control through abstinence.

Research verifies that the length of time a person spends in substance abuse treatment directly influences their recovery outcome and the longer an individual remains abstinent, the less likely they are to relapse. There is no cure for addiction and individuals must continually make an effort and conscious decision to remain abstinent.

Points to Remember

- *Research indicates that the skills individuals learn through cognitive-behavioral therapy remain after the completion of treatment.*

- *Studies demonstrate that incentive-based interventions are highly effective in increasing treatment retention and promoting abstinence from drugs.*

- *Treatment approaches that involve family have better engagement, higher rates of success, and increased aftercare participation.*

- *The most effective treatments address all of an individual's needs not just their drug use.*

- *Combining treatment medications with behavioral therapy is the most successful way to ensure success.*

Part Two:
Behavioral Addictions

Chapter 6

Fighting Against the Odds:
Understanding Gambling Addiction

For many, gambling is a pleasurable activity that creates excitement and anticipation in the participant. Gambling has many variations to include casino slot parlors, table games, and most recently internet-based gambling in the form of fantasy sports and virtual card games. For some individuals, gambling can take on addictive qualities, resulting in financial stress, loss of relationships, and even suicidal ideation in more severe cases (Fauth-Bühler, Mann, & Potenza, 2016).

Gambling is defined as the act of betting on an "uncertain outcome," [or more specifically] "to play a game for money or property" (Merriam-Webster, 2019, n.p.). For a healthy individual, the act of gambling and winning satisfies the reward system in the brain; however, as soon as a loss occurs, the individual becomes less motivated to gamble understanding that the probable loss of money outweighs the benefit of a potential next win. For the individual experiencing gambling addiction, however, the reward system in the brain is activated with effects similar to those of drug abuse (American Psychiatric Association, 2013). This individual craves the act of gambling more and more despite the negative consequences experienced (Smith, 2015).

There are many reasons why an individual becomes addicted to gambling and it cannot be easily explained by brain chemistry; however, it can be said with certainty that not all individuals suffering from gambling addiction will respond to treatment in the same way (National Center for Responsible Gaming, 2012). When working with a client who is addicted to gambling, a practitioner must examine the biological, social, and psychological variables that have influenced the patient's propensity toward this particular addiction (National Center for Responsible Gaming, 2012; Suissa, 2011). It is also necessary to look for markers of other forms of addiction, as substance abuse disorders have a high rate of co-morbidity with gambling addiction (Choliz, 2016).

Gambling as a Disorder

The World Health Organization (1977) first recognized excessive gambling as a psychiatric disorder in the International Classification of Diseases, 9th edition (ICD-9). Just a few years later, the American Psychiatric Association (1980) included excessive gambling in the third edition of the Diagnostic and Statistical Manual of Mental Disorders (DSM-3). It was first classified as an impulse control disorder, being partly described as a disorder in which an individual experiences a progressive loss of control that creates damage to the individual's family, job, and personal interests (Fauth-Bühler et al., 2016).

In the DSM-4 (American Psychiatric Association, 1994), excessive gambling was changed to pathological gambling and was classified under the substance abuse disorder category. The logic was that individuals suffering from pathological gambling could not cut back or stop gambling despite their own efforts (Fauth-Bühler et al., 2016). For many individuals, gambling creates the euphoric-like state similar to that experienced after engaging in substance use (Romanczuk-Seiferth, Koehler, Dreesen, Wüstenberg, & Heinz, 2014).

The most recent edition, the DSM-5 (American Psychiatric Association, 2013), classifies pathological gambling as a substance-related and addictive disorder. The reasoning for this re-classification is based on the similarities between drug addiction and excessive gambling, such as genetic predisposition, treatment response, and biological changes including shifts in cognition (Fauth-Bühler et al., 2016). Upon further examination, however, pathological or excessive gambling shares characteristics of all three categories – impulse control, substance abuse, and addictive disorders.

Impulse Control and Gambling

Although the ICD-10 includes pathological gambling in the same category as such impulse control disorders as pyromania and kleptomania, there is a weak link between the development of gambling addiction and other impulse control disorders (Fauth-Bühler et al., 2016; Grant et al., 2014). The similarities between pathological gambling and other impulse control disorders involve the inability to control behaviors and emotions. An individual engaging in pathological gambling has lost the ability to resist the impulse to gamble, which acts as a type of reward to the individual. Despite the potential loss of money, property, or relationships, the promise of a greater reward keeps the individual addicted (Fauth-Bühler et al., 2016; Grant et al., 2014).

Impulsivity is also defined by both motor response and decision-making impulses (Bakhshani, 2014; Grant et al., 2014). In the case of gambling addiction, the individual cannot inhibit their physical actions when it comes to participating in the act of gambling (e.g., pulling the lever on the slot machine, rolling the dice, going online to the fantasy sports site). There is a weak signal for the individual to stop the behavior, and thus they continue to engage in the behavior impulsively (Fauth-Bühler et al., 2016). Similarly, the addicted individual cannot delay the gratification of rewards and will continue to gamble for smaller, quicker rewards despite the potential for a greater, larger reward down the road (Fauth-Bühler et al., 2016). The individual acts on impulse and does not have the control or foresight necessary to consider other scenarios (Fauth-Bühler et al., 2016).

Along with impulse control difficulties, individuals can also suffer from compulsive actions. Compulsive behaviors are defined as repetitive urges over which an individual has inadequate control, as well as a "tendency to perform repetitive acts in a habitual or stereotyped manner" (Figee et al., 2016, p. 856). In pathological gambling, such compulsions can take the form of lucky rituals before gambling or playing the same slot machine during each visit to the casino (Figgee et al., 2016).

Substance Abuse and Addiction Disorder and Gambling

According to the ICD-10, there are several core elements that must be present in order to diagnose an addiction disorder (Alavi et al., 2012). First, there must be diminished control over reducing or terminating engagement with the addictive substance/behavior despite the individual suffering negative consequences (Sussman et al., 2011). Second, there must be a strong desire or compulsion to engage with the substance/behavior (Sussman et al., 2011). Third, the individual must develop an increased tolerance to the substance/behavior; that is, the individual must need greater or more frequent exposure to the addiction (Sussman et al., 2011). Lastly, an individual must experience withdrawal symptoms when attempting to disengage from the substance/behavior (Sussman et al., 2011). Pathological gambling and substance use disorders share some of these characteristics such as craving and loss of control; however, they also share similar changes in brain structure, specifically within the reward system (Romanczuk-Seiferth et al., 2014).

Substance abuse and addiction disorders are also characterized by an altered function of the reward system in the brain (Fauth-Bühler et al., 2016; Jazaeri & Bin Habil, 2012). In the case of substance abuse, the reward system in the brain is pharmacologically induced into a euphoric state, thus creating the need for more of the substance. In the case of pathological gambling, the actual stimuli associated with the act of gambling (e.g., casino atmosphere, sounds of machines, etc.) have been shown to alter the brain activity of individuals similar to that of substance abuse (Crockford et al., 2005, Goudriaan et al., 2010, & Van Holst et al., 2012). The individual continues to need more exposure to these stimuli in order to obtain the euphoric-like feelings produced by the act and atmosphere of gambling.

Warning Signs

Defined as a social problem, excessive gambling can have a negative impact on families and communities as well as the individual with the disorder (Jazaeri & Bin Habil, 2012). As gambling behavior increases, individuals can suffer a breakdown of community networks, specifically in the form of the deterioration of family units, friendships, and other social connections. In the most severe cases, homelessness and suicidal ideation can occur (Suissa, 2011). Before an individual's addiction gets to a critical level, however, there are several warning signs that friends and family can look for to determine if intervention is warranted.

The following is a list of some of the most common warning signs for gambling addiction. This list is not exhaustive, and family and friends should use their discretion if they suspect a loved one is suffering from a gambling addiction (Mayo Clinic, 2019a):

- A preoccupation with gambling, specifically with a need to find ways to obtain more money for gambling
- Needing increased amounts of money in order to gain the same high
- Unsuccessful attempts to curb or stop gambling
- Using gambling as a means of escape from problems or negative feelings (e.g., guilt, anxiety, depression)
- Attempting to regain lost money by gambling more
- Lying or hiding the extent of gambling
- Putting relationships and jobs at risk in favor of gambling
- Stealing or performing fraudulent activities in order to get more money for gambling
- Looking to others for financial support to pay off gambling debts

It is also important to note that pathological gamblers can experience remission in the severity of symptoms; however, without treatment, these individuals are likely to return to their gambling addiction, especially in the face of other life stressors (Mayo Clinic, 2019a).

Causes

Excessive gambling can be attributed to a myriad of factors to include biological, genetic, and environmental. It is often the result of a combination of these factors that makes it a difficult disorder to treat. Aside from the biological explanations previously described, there are several more abstract explanations as to why some individuals develop gambling addictions. One such explanation places the blame on poor social structures (Abbott et al., 2018). Some studies have concluded that individuals who have deficits in developing appropriate social connections are more likely to crave the perceived acceptance of the social structure of the gambling community (Abbott et al., 2018; Suissa, 2011). For an individual who does not have a healthy understanding of social boundaries, the result can be a dependence on the feeling of belonging, which is only reinforced by the high-like feeling that comes from risk-taking (Brevers & Noël, 2013).

Similarly, some researchers attribute developing gambling addiction to an individual's level of vulnerability (Abbott et al., 2018; Suissa, 2011). Individuals who are susceptible to gambling addiction are often those who are vulnerable members of society; for example, these individuals may live in situations where their freedom of choice is substantially limited (e.g., poverty, domestic abuse). In this case, the prospect of gambling as a means of choice (individuals can choose which games they play, how much they bet, and so on) is attractive (Suissa, 2011). An additional problem is created when these marginalized individuals are most often targeted with gambling propaganda; for example, in poverty-stricken areas, one is likely to see a variety of bars, most of which offer a variety of video gambling options such as Keno or video poker. With the promise of escape from a negative situation, vulnerable individuals who are looking for hope will often partake in these gaming offerings (Pidd, 2017).

A more recent cause of addiction to gambling is thought to be the prevalence of online gambling (Abbott et al., 2018; Choliz, 2016). Although gambling of all types can have addictive properties for the right individual, some forms are more addictive than others and the addictive potential of a specific type of gambling depends on its availability, accessibility, and immediacy of reward (Abbott et al., 2018; Choliz, 2016). With the advent of virtual gambling, accessible both on the computer and on smartphones, pathological gamblers have a new pathway through which to access their addiction. Virtual gambling is available 24 hours a day, 7 days a week, and its accessibility is practically universal given the technological society of the 21st century (Abbott et al., 2018).

One area of virtual gambling, fantasy sports leagues, has experienced an explosion in participants in recent years. In 2017, the Fantasy Sports and Gaming Association (FSGA) stated that approximately 59 million people in both the United States and Canada participated in fantasy sports leagues (McCormick, 2019). The premise of fantasy sports leagues is for an individual to assume the role of a team manager or owner by putting together a virtual roster of real-life athletes, both professional and non-professional (Nower,

Caler, Pickering & Blaszczynski, 2018). The goal is to obtain the most points which are accrued from the athletes' real-life in-game performances (Nower et al., 2018). Although these sports leagues are virtual, the prize money awarded to winners is very real. In 2018, it was estimated that the fantasy sports industry brought in about 2.91 billion U.S. dollars in revenue (Gough, 2019). Some sites pay out approximately 90% of their collected fees in order to keep players returning for more (Wilson, 2016). With these statistics, it is not surprising that players with gambling addictions choose to participate in this form of gaming over other traditional methods.

Risk Factors

Although it is difficult to pinpoint with exact certainty which individuals are likely to develop a gambling addiction, there are several agreed-upon risk factors that are often associated with excessive gambling. While this is not a complete list of risk factors, it is important to recognize that certain individuals may be more susceptible to developing an addiction based on biological, social, and pharmacological influences (Mayo Clinic, 2019a).

Age. Younger and middle-aged people are more likely to participate in excessive gambling; however, if a child or teenager develops gambling behavior, they are more likely to become addicted to gambling later in life. There is evidence that excessive gambling can also be problematic among the elderly population, although it is not as well-studied as younger populations.

Certain medications. Drugs, such as those used to treat restless leg syndrome and Parkinson's disease may have a rare side effect that causes compulsive behaviors, like gambling, in some individuals (Mayo Clinic, 2019a). These drugs, known as dopamine agonists, stimulate the areas of the brain that govern reward, pleasure, and addiction; therefore, when a patient takes these medications, it is often reported that they feel as though they cannot control urges that were not present previously (Weiss & Marsh, 2012).

Existing mental health disorders. There is a high rate of co-morbidity between gambling addiction and substance abuse disorders (Fauth-Bühler et al., 2016; Nower et al., 2018; Romanczuk-Seiferth et al., 2014). There is evidence that excessive gambling may be associated with bipolar disorder and obsessive-compulsive disorder (Suissa, 2011). Some early studies have even suggested that the brains of gambling addicts and children with attention-deficit/hyperactivity disorder (ADHD) have similar neurological functioning deficiencies (Suissa, 2011).

Family/friend influence. Having a friend or family member with a gambling problem increases the risk of developing the same problem in some individuals. There is also evidence that genetics may play a role in developing a gambling addiction (Fauth-Bühler et al., 2016).

Gender. It is more common for men to participate in pathological gambling than for women. In one recent study on predictors of relapse, almost twice as many men than women suffered from excessive gambling (Smith et al., 2015). When women do become addicted, however, it is often later in life and their rate of addiction is often quicker than that of men.

Race. A recent study on gambling addiction and mental health problems suggests that Hispanic and Asian individuals may be at the greatest risk for developing a gambling addiction; yet, these groups are the least likely to find targeted prevention and treatment (Nower et al., 2018).

Personality characteristics. People who are highly competitive, impulsive by nature, restless, easily bored, or who are addicted to less detrimental activities, such as work, may have a propensity toward developing a gambling addiction. The thrill of winning coupled with the inherent risk of gambling can be very difficult to overcome for these individuals.

Negative Effects

The effects of gambling addiction can vary greatly. For some individuals, there are physiological impacts, while for others, the effects may be strictly psychological. Research supports the idea that all pathological gamblers suffer some type of negative consequence in at least one of three domains – biological, psychological, and/or social and may include

Potential Biological/Physiological Impacts

- Increased chance of developing hypertension
- Sleep deprivation/insomnia
- Increased chance of developing cardiovascular disease
- Stomach ulcers
- Headaches
- Higher levels of the stress hormone, cortisol
- Development of substance dependence
- Increased rates of obesity

Potential Psychological Impacts

- Depression
- Feelings of guilt, shame, and desperation

- Increased risk of suicidal ideation

- Anxiety

- Increase in impulsive/compulsive behaviors

- Changes in cognitive functioning

- Distortions in the "fight or flight" mechanisms

Potential Social Impacts

- Financial loss

- Loss of job

- Breaks in relationships

- Divorce

- Increase in crime, specifically theft and fraud

- Bankruptcy

- Homelessness

    (Brevers & Noël, 2013; Choliz, 2016; Fong, 2005; Nower et al., 2018; Smith et al., 2015)

Not all gambling addicts will suffer from the same consequences and the severity of each consequence is dependent upon the individual. Excessive gamblers who have pre-existing conditions, such as depression or bipolar disorder, may experience more severe effects than individuals who have developed an addiction based on sensory-seeking needs (Fong, 2005).

Diagnostic tools can be used as predictors for long-term negative outcomes; for example, if an individual is suspected of having a gambling addiction, a medical history and medication review can often reveal the biological and psychological underpinnings of the addiction (Mayo Clinic, 2019a). From there, practitioners can select treatment options that are best suited to reduce the physiological and psychiatric consequences of the addiction.

Treatment for Gambling Addiction

There are many challenges to treating excessive gambling. One obstacle is that most individuals have a hard time admitting they have a problem. Since gambling is a legal form of entertainment in much of the United States, as well as other countries, it is difficult for addicts to acknowledge a loss of control since they feel as though they are participating in a harmless leisure activity (Choliz, 2016). Whether the addict acknowledges a problem or is pressured into treatment by family and friends, it is important to select the treatment option that best fits the individual. There are many different methods for treating excessive gambling. Sometimes individuals respond to a single treatment method, while others benefit from a combination of options (Mayo Clinic, 2019a). These are some of the most common treatment methods for excessive gambling:

Gamblers Anonymous (GA): GA is a 12-step recovery program designed to provide a fellowship treatment approach for men and women who are ready to admit they have a gambling addiction. GA does not charge membership fees, nor is the organization affiliated with any other recovery program. During the program, individuals admit they have a gambling problem and they commit to working within themselves to understand why gambling has such power. Ideally, individuals attend meetings, as often as they need, where they share their feelings with other excessive gamblers. Meetings are held in every state in the U.S. as well as internationally. Friends and supporters are welcome to attend some of the meetings, but others are reserved for excessive gamblers only. There is an additional organization, Gam-Anon, which supports friends and families through the 12-step process, providing them with a way in which to connect with others who are supporting an excessive gambler. For more information, visit www.gamblersanonymous.org

Medication: Depending upon the underlying reasons for developing a gambling addiction, medication may help relieve some of the symptoms that go along with excessive gambling. Antidepressants and mood stabilizers may help with symptoms of depression, OCD, and ADHD, which can either be precursors to developing an addiction or co-morbid disorders developed with the addiction (Mayo Clinic, 2019a; Suissa, 2011). Selective serotonin reuptake inhibitors (SSRIs) have been shown to have a positive impact on reducing the symptoms of gambling addiction. This class of drugs helps reduce the impulsivity in excessive gamblers, allowing them to maintain some control over their desire to gamble (Lupi et al. 2014).

More intensive medications, such as lithium, have shown some levels of effectiveness in treating excessive gambling when taken as a treatment for co-morbid bipolar disorder symptoms; however, it should be noted that research on the effectiveness of medication to treat gambling addiction is ongoing (Fauth-Bühler, 2016). Until the neurobiological mechanisms are better understood, it is difficult to determine whether medication is treating the actual addiction or the related symptoms that develop alongside it (Lupi et al., 2014).

Therapy: Both cognitive behavior therapy (CBT) and exposure therapy have shown positive results in treating excessive gambling. CBT is a form of therapy that aims to reframe negative thought patterns and the associated behaviors (Young, Mumby, & Smolinski, 2019). CBT works on the idea that patients can change their behavior through a more positive thought process. In the case of excessive gambling, patients engaged in CBT would participate in individual therapy sessions in which they would be assigned "semi-structured homework assignments ... [as a means] to facilitate practice and reinforcement of the skills learned during the week's session" (Okuda et al., 2009, p. 1326). Over time, patients are expected to learn their gambling triggers, feelings and thoughts associated with gambling, and develop the skills to evaluate the consequences of engaging in gambling behavior (Okuda et al., 2009).

Exposure therapy, on the other hand, is a form of treatment developed to help people overcome their fears, or in this case, addictions, by slowly exposing them to the situation over which they feel powerless (Young, Mumby, & Smolinski, 2019). Exposure therapy can help with excessive gambling by helping to reduce the urge to compulsively gamble when presented with gambling-related cues (e.g., casino lights, noises, smells) (Grant et al., 2014). This exposure therapy can be performed in vivo (directly facing the situation in real life), imaginal (vividly reimaging the situation), virtual reality (using virtual reality technology to recreate the situation), or interoceptive (intentionally bringing on the sensations of the situations in a safe environment) (American Psychological Association, n.d.b). Practitioners and patients together would choose which method is most likely to be the safest and most effective. The goal is to expose the patient to the situation or stimuli in order to decrease their adverse response. In the case of excessive gambling, the goal would be to slowly expose the patient to gambling situations and teach them skills to recognize and reduce the urges to gamble (Grant et al., 2014).

Final Thoughts

There are over 1,000 casinos in the United States alone and as of 2016, approximately 2.6% of Americans had a gambling problem (North American Foundation for Gambling Addiction, 2017). That number has likely increased due to the prevalence of online gaming and fantasy sports leagues. With approximately 16% of the U.S. and Canadian population engaging in online gambling, it is important to remain aware of the warning signs and risk factors, both individually and in others, for developing a gambling addiction (Nower et al., 2018).

If an individual is suspected of having a gambling problem, there are many options to help family and friends determine if their loved one is at risk. Those who support addicts in finding a rehabilitation solution should check the warning signs, examine the individual's medical and medication history, identify life stressors that may be contributing to a gambling problem, and seek treatment options. With multiple treatment options available, it is possible for individuals to overcome a gambling addiction.

Points to Remember

- *For individuals experiencing gambling addiction, the reward center in the brain is activated with effects similar to those of drug abuse.*

- *The causes of excessive gambling are not easily determined and can be the result of biological, psychological, or social factors.*

- *Gambling addiction has markers of three types of disorders: impulse control disorders, substance abuse, and addictive disorders.*

- *Excessive gambling can result in a plethora of negative consequences, the most severe being suicide, homelessness, and crime.*

- *Treatment for excessive gambling varies by individual, the most successful options being 12-step programs, medication, and therapy.*

Chapter 7

Fighting the Struggle Within:

Understanding Food Addiction

Food is both essential for survival and the source of pleasure for many; however, for people who suffer from compulsive eating, food is often seen as a comfort from negative emotions or low self-esteem (Weinstein, Zlatkes, Gingis, & Lejoyeux, 2015). Unfortunately, when an individual uses food to deal with negative emotions, they may inadvertently trigger more negative emotions with regard to their compulsive eating. Eating then becomes a vicious cycle, one in which individuals are often powerless to break. Eating is crucial for survival; yet, excessive consumption of food can cause a host of biological, psychological, and social problems (Weinstein et al., 2015).

As of 2018, the obesity epidemic affected approximately 42.4% of American individuals and severe obesity has increased from 4.7% to 9.2% in less than 20 years (Hales, Carroll, Fryar & Ogden, 2020). While there are several elements that influence an individual's propensity toward obesity (such as biological, genetic, and environmental concerns), researchers speculate that the addictive-like properties of some foods can be a contributing factor (Berenson, Laz, Pohlmeier, Rahman, & Cunningham, 2015; Gordon, Ariel-Donges, Bauman, & Merlo, 2018). Studies suggest that certain hyperpalatable foods (foods that are high in sugar, fat, and salt) can have addictive properties since consuming them results in increased dopamine levels in the brain (Berenson et al., 2015).

Researchers have not come to a consensus over whether or not food addiction is a real behavioral addiction as it is difficult to measure; therefore, there has not been one particular assessment to determine the presence of food addiction (Gordon et al., 2018). In 2009, the Yale Food Addiction Scale (YFAS) was developed to assess whether an individual exhibits patterns of consumption of highly palatable foods in a manner consistent with substance dependence (Berenson et al., 2015). Studies since have suggested that food addiction affects approximately 8.4% of women aged 45-64, and 2.7% of women aged 62-88 (Flint, Gearhardt, Corbin, Brownell, Field, & Rimm, 2014). It is important to mention, however, that food addiction is not necessarily synonymous with obesity, with many healthy-weight individuals reporting symptoms of food addiction that have not led to weight gain (Gordon et al., 2018).

Food Addiction: Is it Really a Disorder?

Researchers have been hesitant to label food addiction as a legitimate behavioral addiction. While there is no official diagnosis of addiction in clinical practice, the American Psychological Association (n.d.c) has described addiction as

> *A chronic disorder with biological, psychological, social and environmental factors influencing its development and maintenance. About half the risk for addiction is genetic. Genes affect the degree of reward that individuals experience when initially using a substance (e.g., drugs) or engaging in certain behaviors (e.g., gambling), as well as the way the body processes alcohol or other drugs. Heightened desire to re-experience use of the substance or behavior potentially influenced by psychological (e.g., stress, history of trauma), social (e.g., family or friends' use of a substance) and environmental factors (e.g., accessibility of a substance, low cost) can lead to regular use/exposure, with chronic use/exposure leading to brain changes* (n.p.).

Addiction, therefore, most closely aligns with severe substance use disorders (Gordon et al., 2018). This may be why researchers cannot agree on whether food addiction fits into this category. Food must be consumed for survival; therefore, it is difficult to discern whether or not it can also be categorized as a "substance" that can be abused to the point of addiction.

While the Diagnostic and Statistical Manual of Mental Disorders, 5th Edition (DSM-5) (American Psychiatric Association, 2013) does not officially recognize food addiction, Meule and Gearhardt (2014) posit that at least four of the 11 criteria for substance use disorders are empirically supported, while the other criteria are plausible. Adapted from the DSM-5 (American Psychiatric Association, 2013) by Gordon et al. (2018), the following criteria for substance abuse disorder:

- *Consuming a substance in greater amounts over longer periods of time than intended*

- *Having a persistent desire or unsuccessfully attempting to decrease or limit substance abuse*

- *Spending a significant amount of time acquiring, using, or recovering from a substance*

- *Craving the substance or having a strong urge to use it*

- *Being unable to fulfill obligations at work, school, or home due to use of a substance*

- *Continually using a substance despite its effects causing or exacerbating persistent or recurrent social or interpersonal problems*

- *Giving up or reducing social, occupational, or recreational activities due to substance use*

- *Continually using a substance in situations in which it is physically dangerous (e.g., driving under the influence of a substance)*

- *Continually using a substance despite physical or psychological problems that are caused or made worse by the substance use*

- *Needing a substantially higher dose of the substance in order to achieve the desired effect, or experiencing substantially reduced effect of the substance when the usual dose is consumed*

- *Experiencing negative physical and psychological symptoms when the substance is not consumed at the typical dose*

(p. 449).

According to Meule & Gearhardt (2014), tweaking the wording to allow for a food addiction, the equivalents are empirically supported as occurring in individuals suffering from excessive food consumption.

- Food often consumed in larger amounts or over a longer period than was intended

- Persistent desire of unsuccessful efforts to cut down or control food intake

- Craving, or a strong desire or urge to eat specific foods

- Overeating is continued despite knowledge of having a persistent or recurrent physical or psychological problem that is likely to have been caused or exacerbated by overeating foods

The following possible food addiction equivalents are plausible in those who consume excess food:

- Great deal of time is spent in activities necessary to obtain or overeat foods or recover from its effects

- Recurrent overeating resulting in a failure to fulfill major role obligations at work, school, or home

- Continued overeating despite having persistent or recurrent social or interpersonal problems caused or exacerbated by the effects of specific foods

- Important social, occupational, or recreational activities are given up or reduced due to overeating foods

- Recurrent overeating in situation in which it is physically hazardous
- Need for markedly increased amounts of food to achieve desired effect
- Withdrawal symptoms when refraining from eating specific foods (Meule & Gearhardt, 2014).

While all of these criteria could be considered indicators of food addiction, there are other factors to consider. Obesity and binge eating, although they do share some commonalities with food addiction, are not caused by the same factors. Studies have suggested that only 24.9% of overweight or obese individuals have reported clinically significant symptoms of food addiction (Gordon et al., 2018; Pursey, Stanwell, Gearhardt, Collins, & Burrows, 2014). Similarly, 11.1% of healthy-weight individuals have reported symptoms of food addiction, suggesting that food addiction does not necessarily cause obesity (Gordon et al., 2018). Obesity can also be attributed to other factors such as genetics, environmental challenges (lack of access to nutritionally dense foods), and other biological influences (medication, certain health conditions) (Gordon et al., 2018).

Binge eating disorder (BED), a disorder in which individuals frequently consume unusually large amounts of food and feel unable to stop eating, differs from food addiction in that only 56.8% of individuals suffering from BED report clinically significant symptoms of food addiction (Gordon et al., 2018; Long, Blundell, & Finlayson, 2015; Mayo Clinic, 2019b). In contrast to food addiction, individuals suffering from BED do not necessarily binge on only hyperpalatable foods. Binge eaters may continue to eat long after they are full due to the inability to stop the urge to eat, not necessarily because the food tastes good (Mayo Clinic, 2019b).

As with other addictions, it is difficult to pinpoint whether it is the food that has addictive properties or if the compulsive eating is the response to an underlying mental health condition (Weinstein et al., 2015). Individuals who suffer from food addiction are likely to also exhibit symptoms of depression and anxiety; however, it is often difficult to figure out which had the earlier onset (Weinstein et al., 2015). Compulsive eating can be both the cause and result of several biological, psychological, and social challenges and this is especially true for children who exhibit symptoms of food addiction and/or BED. Children who suffer from low self-esteem, depression, and exhibit heightened externalizing behaviors are more likely to report food addiction symptoms (Carlisle, Buser, & Carlisle, 2012; Ogundele, 2018).

Warning Signs

While food addiction appears to be a predominately Western society issue, mainly due to the availability of hyperpalatable and nutritionally empty foods, it can impact anyone, although females seem to be more susceptible to developing the addiction than males (Berenson et al., 2015; Gunnars, 2019a). In addition to negative physical impacts, food addiction can also have social and psychological impacts. There are at least eight symptoms that are typical of food addicts, although not all individuals will exhibit the same signs and symptoms or to the same degree (Gunnars, 2019a):

- Despite being full, a craving is present
- Eating much more than was originally intended
- Eating until feeling excessively full
- Feelings of guilt after eating to excess, yet doing it repeatedly
- Making up excuses for excessive eating
- Repeated failures at setting rules surrounding food and eating
- Hiding eating behaviors from others
- Inability to quit despite physical problems

Unfortunately, for someone who is addicted to food, the rule of abstinence doesn't work. Everyone needs to eat to survive; therefore, the idea of abstaining from food is not realistic. Abstaining from specific foods, however, can help food addicts control some of their compulsive eating behaviors. For food addicts, moderation doesn't work (Gunnars, 2019a). Keeping hyperpalatable or trigger foods in the house can be enough to cause an episode of compulsive eating. While everyone has cravings and may indulge in a "cheat meal" here or there, it becomes problematic when an individual's daily life is consumed by the thoughts and actions of eating to excess.

Causes

Although controversial in its existence as a true addiction, researchers have suggested some possible reasons why individuals may develop addictive-like responses to food. Some possible factors influencing food addiction are hyperpalatable foods, operant conditioning to engage more frequently in compulsive eating, mood and stress, food cues, cravings, and impulsivity (Kalon, Hong, Tobin, & Schulte, 2016).

Hyperpalatable foods. Certain types of food are considered hyperpalatable due to their increased combination of fat, salt, and/or sugar (University of Kansas, 2019). These foods are thought to have addictive properties due to their high levels of additives (Berenson et al., 2015; Kalon et al., 2016). Research suggests that it is not only the act of eating these foods that can trigger food addiction, merely viewing pictures of highly palatable foods or drinks have triggered the reward centers of the brain (Gearhardt et al., 2011).

Operant conditioning. As with drug addiction, the evolution of addictive eating may be best explained by the individual's increase in using the food to avoid withdrawal symptoms (Kalon et al., 2016). At first, the individual occasionally indulges in high-calorie foods as a means of eliciting a pleasurable feeling; however, as times goes on, the individual is more likely to indulge in the food as a means of escaping the adverse reactions that accompany abstinence from a certain type of food (Kalon et al., 2016). What was once a rewarding experience has become a necessary mechanism for avoiding unpleasant physical sensations.

Mood and stress. Like other addictions, compulsive eating may be linked to the inability to cope with negative emotions. Individuals who experience food addiction are likely to experience negative affect, mood dysregulation, weight cycling, body dissatisfaction, and fear of self-compassion (Kalon et al., 2016). In fact, for individuals who experience these difficulties, food can act as both a balm and an irritant. Individuals overeat to feel comfort, yet the guilt they often feel afterwards creates a depressive state wherein low self-esteem and poor self-image is the result (Berenson et al., 2015).

Food cues. Individuals with healthy eating patterns can often discern whether or not their cravings are the result of a negative mood, but for those suffering from food addiction, it is often difficult to shift their focus from eating an unhealthy meal. Research suggests that states of mood impact the attention that individuals give to food cues (Frayn, Sears, & von Ranson, 2016; Kalon et al., 2016). Individuals with a food addiction are often unlikely to choose a healthy food choice after they have experienced a sad mood. Research has suggested that this is due to the reward networks in the brain being activated and reactivated in response to the unhealthy food choice; and therefore, food addiction has a neurobiological component similar to other addictions (Kalon et al., 2016).

Cravings. For individuals who enjoy hyperpalatable foods, the strength of cravings may be more intense than for people who do not regularly eat these types of foods. Cravings are often activated by emotions; therefore, it can be easy for a food addict to begin to crave high fat, sugary, or salty foods that once connected to a specific emotion (Joyner, Gearhardt, & White, 2015). Cravings are not always the result of negative emotions. They can also be attributed to positive emotions, such as happy memories that involved food consumption (e.g., a celebration with food). Research suggests, however, that cravings can be a partial predictor of compulsive eating and higher weight in individuals suffering from food addiction (Joyner et al., 2015).

Impulsivity. Similar to other addictions, impulsivity has been thought to have a direct correlation to the development of food addiction. Impulsive individuals lack the foresight and planning necessary to act with caution; therefore, impulsive food addicts will often engage in pleasure-seeking behavior without the thought of potential negative consequences (Kalon et al., 2016). Unfortunately, impulsivity doesn't only lead to food addiction, but also to other eating disorders such as binge eating disorder and bulimia nervosa (Kalon et al., 2016). Impulsivity has its roots in neurobiological dysfunction; therefore, it can be seen as a brain disorder. Individuals who exhibit impulse control around food have little or no control over managing their food intake without treatment.

What is perhaps most challenging for food addicts is that they are surrounded by food at all times. Food addicts are often not aware of their trigger foods, which further complicates matters. Keeping these foods within reach only exacerbates the problem, creating easy access to the addictive substance (Food Addicts Anonymous, n.d.). Individuals who are addicted to food can find some relief in abstinence of those trigger foods, but often need further treatment to avoid relapse (Food Addicts Anonymous, n.d.).

Risk Factors

Although there is not yet an agreement as to whether food addiction is an actual mental health disorder, there are several risk factors associated with developing eating disorders in general. Since food addiction is ostensibly an eating disorder, risk factors that are seen in individuals with other types of eating disorders are often seen in those who suffer from addictive eating.

Psychological risk factors. For individuals who suffer from underlying psychological disorders, such as depression, anxiety, and obsessive-compulsive disorders, compulsive eating can often act as a comfort. When an individual has poor coping mechanisms, they often turn to substances or actions that block negative emotions (Berenson et al., 2015; Kalon et al., 2016; Weinstein et al., 2015). In the case of food addiction, the food functions similar to a drug in that eating it provides a much-needed release of dopamine for the individual suffering from the mental health disorder. As time goes on, however, the individual requires more of the substance to achieve the same feeling (Meule & Gearhardt, 2014). As a result, the individual begins to suffer from increased depression and anxiety due to the inability to control eating patterns or stop troubling physical symptoms (Gordon et al., 2018).

For individuals who suffer from bulimia, a binge eating disorder, the idea of achieving perfectionism can often be the reason why food addiction morphs into a binge/purge cycle. Individuals who have both body image issues and difficulty controlling themselves around food are more likely to develop eating disorders (National Eating Disorders Association, 2018).

Sociocultural risk factors. In today's culture, the perceived idea of being perfectly thin is everywhere (National Eating Disorders Association, 2018). Advertisements, especially those targeting women, generally feature models who seem impossibly thin. In fact, most advertisements rely heavily on digital enhancements to create this ideal. In Western society, particularly in the United States, the idea of the thin body being the only acceptable body type leads to increased body dissatisfaction (Roberts & Roberts, 2015). For those women who internalize the idea that to be happy means to be thin, food addiction is particularly problematic. This often leads to excessive or yo-yo dieting, which can have negative impacts on health (National Eating Disorders Association, 2018).

As a result of the pressure put on women to maintain an impossibly slender body, food addicts who cannot control their caloric intake, and therefore cannot maintain a healthy weight, are often at a higher risk of avoiding social situations in which they may be judged for their eating habits and/or weight (National Eating Disorders Association, 2018). This may also promote further depressive symptoms, as the individual feels helpless over their behavior.

Biological risk factors. For individuals with a family history of an eating disorder and/or depression, anxiety, or other addiction disorder, the likelihood of developing an eating disorder is increased (National Alliance on Mental Illness, n.d.). The same holds true for individuals who suffer from a disorder in which eating must be closely monitored, such as Celiac disease or food allergies. For individuals with Type 2 diabetes, research has shown there is a correlation between the disease and food addiction (Yang et al., 2017). Compulsive eating is a characteristic of Type 2 diabetes; yet, there is also evidence pointing to food addiction as being an existing disorder prior to the diagnosis of Type 2 diabetes (Yang et al., 2017). It is not yet clear if there are other illnesses directly related to compulsive eating; however, the possibility of food addiction as a contributing factor in many negative health conditions has been suggested.

Negative Effects

The effects of food addiction can vary depending on the individual. While there are almost always psychological symptoms associated with food addiction, there can also be harmful physical consequences of compulsive eating. No matter which symptoms the individual experiences, there is always a diminished quality of life associated with food addiction (Klimek, 2016). According to the American Addiction Centers (n.d.b), Klimek (2016) and the National Eating Disorder Association (n.d.), these include

Potential Physical and Health Impacts

- Heart attack or stroke
- High blood pressure and cholesterol
- Kidney disease and/or failure
- Arthritis and/or bone deterioration
- Sleep apnea
- Weight gain

Potential Psychological Impacts

- Major depression
- Generalized anxiety disorder
- Social phobias
- Mood dysregulation
- Body dysmorphic disorder
- Fear of self-compassion
- Feelings of worthlessness

Potential Social Impacts

- Feeling the need to avoid social situations for fear of judgment
- Feeling the need to hide the amount of food one is consuming
- Fractured relationships (family, friends, work acquaintances)

Although not everyone who exhibits an addictive relationship with food will experience the same symptoms, it is important for family and friends to take notice of both the warning signs and negative effects of food addiction if they suspect their loved one is suffering from compulsive eating (American Addiction Centers, n.d.b). There has not yet been one specific diagnostic tool designed to diagnose food addiction, although the Yale Food Addiction Scale comes close and is the most widely used assessment (Gearhardt, Corbin, & Brownwell, 2009).

Treatment for Food Addiction

Many individuals attempt to remediate the problem on their own and end up experiencing failure time and time again. Others are embarrassed and decide they would rather deal with their addiction than seek help. With any addiction, however, it is almost impossible to heal without support from others. While the scope of treatment for food addiction is not wide, there are several options for those looking for help with compulsive eating (Gunnars, 2019b).

Twelve-Step Programs

Similar to other addictions, there has been evidence that 12-step programs are effective at treating compulsive eating. Perhaps the most well-known program for food addiction, Overeaters Anonymous (n.d.) acts on principles similar to Alcoholics Anonymous. Individuals who join similar programs follow the 12 guiding principles, admitting that they are powerless over their addiction and submit to a higher power (Overeaters Anonymous, n.d.). These types of programs are not professional in nature; rather they consist of members who have worked the principles and found success. Part of the program involves pairing up with a sponsor who has been successful in the program (Overeaters Anonymous, n.d.). Organizations such as Overeaters Anonymous also have their own literature which targets the addiction at the center of the program. Similar programs include Greysheeters Anonymous, Food Addicts in Recovery Anonymous, and Food Addicts Anonymous also offer a similar program structure (Gunnars, 2019b).

Cognitive Behavioral Therapy

For some individuals, Cognitive Behavioral Therapy (CBT) has shown promise as a method of treating food addiction. While most practitioners who work with food addicts treat specific eating disorders (e.g. anorexia nervosa, bulimia nervosa, binge eating disorder), the same tenets of CBT appear to be effective at treating food addiction (Gunnars, 2019b). CBT for compulsive eaters focuses on the belief that the disorder stems from the individual's obsession with meeting societal expectations with regard to body shape and image (Murphy, Straebler, Cooper, & Fairburn, 2010).

Individuals who become preoccupied with meeting a false ideal, and then find they cannot achieve that ideal, become part of a cycle wherein they make rules around food and break them almost immediately (Murphy et al., 2010). This cycle results in the individual's depressed mood over the inability to control their food intake, and subsequently, their over-reliance on the food as a coping mechanism. The treatment phase of CBT focuses on maintaining cognitive and behavioral changes through a series of sequenced therapeutic procedures (Murphy et al., 2010).

Commercial Treatment Programs

There are several treatment centers which focus solely on helping those with eating disorders (Gunnars, 2019b). While not specific to food addiction, these treatment facilities help individuals with all types of eating disorders, such as bulimia, anorexia, orthorexia, and binge eating disorder. Food addiction may be central to treatment, specifically for those who suffer from binge eating disorder. Many of these facilities offer residential programs wherein the individual participates in on-site counseling, activities with others in recovery, and in some cases, spiritual wellness. Treatment facilities can be found across the United States, as well as abroad. Some of the more well-known programs include

- Shift-Recovery by ACORN (https://foodaddiction.com/)
- Milestones in Recovery (https://www.milestonesprogram.org/)
- Shades of Hope (https://shadesofhope.com/)
- Timberline Knolls (https://www.timberlineknolls.com/)

Drug Treatment

Some research suggests that drug treatment may be effective in reducing the symptoms of food addiction in some individuals (Gunnars, 2019b). For individuals with various eating disorders which may be related to food addiction (binge eating disorder and bulimia), certain classes of drugs have shown promise in curbing symptoms. For example, in patients suffering from bulimia, selective serotonin reuptake inhibitors (SSRIs), tri-cyclic antidepressants, anti-convulsants, and even anti-emetic drugs have shown varying degrees of effectiveness in helping one to manage the symptoms of compulsive eating (Gorla & Matthews, 2005).

Prescription appetite suppressants have been used recently for patients suffering from obesity related to poorly-controlled appetite. Drugs such as orlistat and phentermine-topiramate may help individuals control appetite; however, it is important for individuals to talk over the risks and benefits with their doctor before taking these medications as there can be serious or even life-threatening side effects for some people (National Institutes of Health, 2016).

Final Thoughts

Although there are many questions surrounding the merit of a food addiction as a true mental health disorder, for those suffering from an inability to control their eating habits, the condition is a reality from which escape can seem impossible. Regardless of its origins, there is little doubt that food addiction can ultimately contribute to conditions such as obesity, as well as a host of eating disorders. Unfortunately, factors such as ease of access to food and increasingly faster and less expensive options for people on the go are not helping to reduce the number of people affected by food addiction. In 2018, there were over 240,000 fast-food restaurants in the United States (Statista, 2019). This was approximately 4,000 more restaurants than the previous year and 30,000 from a decade ago (Statista, 2019). While food addiction is not the fault of fast food establishments, their prevalence can make it difficult for compulsive eaters to deal with their addiction when food is so readily available.

If an individual is suspected of having a food addiction or other eating disorder, there are several options available. Checking the warning signs and determining if the individual's behavior around food rises to the level of concern is an important first step in intervention. Additionally, monitoring a loved one's emotional state, specifically around food, is another crucial piece of assessing their need for help. As research continues in the area of food addiction, there are likely to be more treatment options available, as well as a lessening of the stigma around compulsive eating.

Points to Remember

- *Researchers have not come to a consensus over whether or not food addiction is a real behavioral addiction.*

- *Food must be consumed for survival; therefore, it is difficult to discern whether or not it can also be categorized as a "substance" which can be abused to the point of addiction.*

- *It is impossible to abstain from food so treatment via the abstinence model is not an option.*

- *Hyperpalatable foods, mood and stress, and cravings are factors that are associated with causing food addiction.*

- *Food addiction appears to have psychological, biological, and sociocultural risk factors.*

- *Most individuals find success with 12-step programs or therapy treatments.*

Chapter 8

When Pleasure Becomes Pain: Understanding Sex Addiction

In today's society, sexual overtones are present everywhere. Television has become more risqué than ever, and advertising continues to push the boundaries of what is socially and morally acceptable through the use of scantily-clad models and racy photographs (Business News Daily, 2020). For most individuals, these visuals are just a part of the 21st century landscape. For some men and women, however, readily-accessible, sexually-explicit materials can be problematic (Anthony, 2018). For these individuals, sex has become an addiction that is difficult to avoid.

There is a recognized biological need for sex between individuals. Sex serves as both a pleasurable activity and a means of reproduction, but for some people, sex can have addictive qualities that interfere in daily functioning. There has been an increase in the number of people reporting excessive sexual thoughts and behaviors (Briggs, Gough, & das Nair, 2017). These individuals describe a compulsion and obsessiveness around sexual behaviors that often interferes with daily life (Briggs et al., 2017). It can be difficult for these individuals to focus on anything other than the act or quest of finding sex, which can create a host of psychological and social challenges (Anthony, 2018).

Unfortunately, experts have not yet come to an agreement around the validity of sexual compulsion as a true addiction disorder (Hall, 2014). Individuals suffering from compulsive sexual thoughts and behavior often report that they feel out of control. Perhaps due to moral and societal beliefs around sex, however, these individuals are often viewed as inherently damaged in some way (Hall, 2014; Phillips, Hajela, & Hilton, 2015). Questions abound as to whether those suffering from sexually compulsive behaviors are making excuses for their behaviors, have poor impulse control, have deeply unmet needs stemming from trauma, or are suffering from other underlying mental health disorders that create sex addiction as a symptom (Hall, 2014).

Sex Addiction: Is it Really a Disorder?

Researchers have not yet come up with answers to questions regarding sex addiction as a true mental health disorder, and more studies are needed in the areas of diagnosis and treatment (Rosenberg, Carnes, & O'Connor, 2014). There is evidence, however, that supports the differentiation between individuals who take part in unorthodox sexual behaviors and those who are truly suffering from compulsive actions (Rosenberg et al., 2014). Over the past few decades, researchers have attempted to propose criteria that would delineate sexual addiction; for example, Goodman (1997) proposed that sex addiction be described as a "maladaptive pattern of sexual behavior that leads to clinically significant impairment or distress, as manifested by three…[criteria], that occur at any time in the same 12-month period" (p. 340). Goodman (1997) shared seven diagnostic criteria that are based on the standard criteria for substance abuse disorders and include

- *Markedly increased amount or intensity of the sexual behavior to achieve the desired effect or a markedly diminished effect with continued involvement in the sexual behavior at the same level of intensity.*

- *Characteristic psychophysiological withdrawal syndrome of physiologically described changes and/or psychologically described changes on discontinuation of sexual behavior or engaging in the same (or closely related) sexual behavior to relieve or avoid withdrawal symptoms.*

- *The sexual behavior is often engaged in over a longer period, in greater quantity, or at a higher level of intensity than was intended.*

- *There is a persistent desire, and efforts to cut down or control the sexual behavior are not successful.*

- *A great deal of time spent on activities necessary to prepare for the sexual behavior, to engage in the behavior, or to recover from its effects.*

- *Important social, occupational, or recreational activities are given up or reduced due to the sexual behavior.*

- *The sexual behavior continues despite knowledge of having a persistent or recurrent physical or psychological problem that is likely to have been caused or exacerbated by the behavior.*

    (p. 341).

Similarly, Carnes et al. (2012) proposed 10 diagnostic criteria for sexual addiction, of which three must be present, to include

- *Recurrent failure to resist impulses to engage in specific sexual behavior*

- *Frequent engaging in sexual behaviors to a greater extent or over a longer period of time than intended*

- *Persistent desire or unsuccessful efforts to stop, reduce, or control sexual behaviors*

- *Inordinate amount of time spent in obtaining sex, being sexual, or recovering from sexual experience*

- *Preoccupation with sexual behavior or preparatory activities*

- *Frequent engaging in sexual behavior when expected to fulfill occupational, academic, domestic, or social obligations*

- *Continuation of sexual behavior despite knowledge or having a persistent or recurrent social, financial, psychological, or physical problem that is caused or exacerbated by the behavior*

- *Need to increase the intensity, frequency, number, or risk of sexual behaviors to achieve the desired effect, or diminished effect with continued sexual behaviors at the same level of intensity, frequency, number, or risk*

- *Giving up or limiting social, occupational, or recreational activities due to sexual behavior*

- *Distress, anxiety, restlessness, or irritability if unable to engage in sexual behavior*

(p. 10).

Carnes et al. (2012), purported that sex addiction affects between 3-6% of the population, but as there are no set criteria for diagnosing the condition, it is difficult to assess. The DSM-5 (American Psychiatric Association, 2013) does not officially recognize sex addiction. There were workgroups who were considering two areas related to sex addiction – Sexual and Gender Identity Disorder and Addiction and Related Disorders; however, sex addiction itself did not make it into the DSM-5 (American Psychiatric Association, 2013), although hypersexual disorder may be considered for the next edition (Rosenberg et al., 2014).

Another obstacle for researchers in determining the validity of sex addiction as a disorder is the high accessibility of sexually-explicit materials through the internet, as well as the increasingly prevalent adult hook-up sites in which individuals can meet up for casual sex through the use of an app (Woehler, Giordano, & Hagedom, 2018). Perhaps most concerning with internet pornography being so readily available is that adolescents are becoming exposed to sexually stimulating materials at earlier ages.

According to the American Psychological Association (2017), the age at which males are first exposed to pornography is significantly associated with their sexual attitudes later in life. In a study of 330 undergraduate men between the ages of 17 and 54 years of age presented at the 125th Annual Convention of the American Psychological Association, the average first exposure to pornography was 13.3 years of age (American Psychological Association, 2017). Early exposure creates a type of split in outcomes later in life. For some men, viewing pornography at young ages reinforces sex roles and beliefs about women. (American Psychological Association, 2017). For young men who predominantly utilize the internet for viewing pornography, the addictive properties of both the internet and the sexually-explicit material can interfere with the reward center in the brain; therefore, creating the setting wherein these individuals need to engage in viewing pornography more and more to cause feelings of excitement (Woehler et al., 2018).

There is also the question of whether or not labeling sex addiction as a mental health disorder will take away an individual's responsibility for their morally questionable behavior. Criticisms of sex addiction proclaim that acceptable sexual behavior is based on moral and social constructs, not science; therefore, there is no way to say that an individual who engages in questionable, high-frequency sexual actions is actually suffering from an addiction (Dodgson, 2017; Phillips et al., 2015). There is research, however, that points to sex addiction as a sort of chemical dependency addiction, similar to food addiction (Phillips et al., 2015). Unlike other behavioral addictions, both food and sex addiction are rooted in the motivation for individual and collective survival. Unfortunately, individuals with a propensity toward addiction develop maladaptive patterns around these behaviors, causing biological, psychological, and social consequences (Berenson et al., 2015; Weinstein et al., 2015).

The Six-Types of Sex Addicts

Even though there is no widely-recognized or scientifically accepted definition of sex addiction at this time, individuals suffering from the markers of sex addiction can present in several different ways. According to Weiss (2019), founder and president of the American Association for Sex Addiction Therapy, there are six specific types of sex addicts who present in very different ways.

Biological Addiction

Someone who is biologically addicted to sex experiences excessive masturbation usually while viewing pornography. These two actions in conjunction work on the basis of classical conditioning wherein the two stimuli are paired, creating a response elicited by both stimuli that eventually turns into being produced by the first stimulus alone (McLeod, 2018). Essentially, the overuse of pornography paired with masturbation creates a type of imprint on the brain. Now the individual has made an association between the pornography and endorphin release from sexual gratification. As a result, the individual may have difficulties functioning sexually within relationships.

Psychological Addiction

For individuals who have suffered from past neglect or abuse, sex can often act as medicine to help with the pain surrounding past unresolved issues (Weiss, 2019). Individuals in this category often indulge in the fantasy of sex, perhaps reveling in others' admiration and desire (Weiss, 2019). This fantasy world often acts as an escape from reality from past hurtful experiences, and the relief that the individuals get from living this way becomes more and more necessary.

Spiritual Addiction

These individuals use sex as a means of looking for a spiritual connection (Weiss, 2019). They only feel spiritually fulfilled when engaging in sexual behaviors. These individuals may be searching for acceptance and love; yet, they have not developed the ability to find it in healthy ways (Weiss, 2019). Unfortunately, the spiritual awakening that is experienced when engaging in sexual behaviors only helps in the short term.

Trauma-Based Sex Addiction

These individuals have experienced a sexual trauma as a child or adolescent and, as a result, they are unable to change their sexual behaviors (Weiss, 2019). Most victims of sexual trauma who experience sexually-addictive behaviors often engage in behaviors that are similar to the trauma; for example, if a young girl was used as a sex object for an older male, she will likely act in ways that perpetuate that trauma when she is older, perhaps by engaging in sex acts with older men or objectifying herself through sexual promiscuity (Weiss, 2019).

Intimacy Anorexia Sex Addiction

People who suffer from intimacy anorexia are addicted to withholding sexual intimacy from their partner or spouse (Weiss, 2019). As a result, the relationship often becomes more like two roommates living together than a marriage or domestic partnership. According to Weiss (2019), someone suffering from intimacy anorexia would be a partner who would "withhold love, withhold praise or appreciation, control by silence/anger, criticism causing isolation, withholding sex, blaming the partner for everything, staying busy to avoid partner time, control/shame with money issues, unable to share feelings, withholding spiritual connection" (n.p.).

Mood Disorder Sex Addiction

Individuals suffering from this type of addiction also suffer from an underlying mental health condition, such as depression and anxiety (Weiss, 2019). The sexual behaviors and subsequent feelings act to alleviate the chemical imbalance due to the mood disorder (Weiss, 2019). Without professional counseling and/or medication therapy, these individuals will likely continue to use sexual behavior to medicate themselves.

It is possible, even probable, that an individual will fit into more than one category of sex addiction. Oftentimes, the underlying causes of the addiction are complex, resulting in the presentation of symptoms in a multitude of ways (Weiss, 2019). It is important to note that just as there are different types of sex addicts, so too are there different types of sex addictions. While there are no distinct, widely-accepted categories, individuals can become addicted to pornography, prostitution, masturbation, fantasy, sadistic or sadomasochistic behavior, exhibition, voyeurism, or other excessive sexual pursuits (American Addiction Centers, 2019b).

Warning Signs of Sex Addiction

While researchers suggest that males are more susceptible to sex addiction than females, the disorder can affect both genders in similar ways (Rosenberg et al., 2014). Sex addiction can have biological, psychological and social impacts, although not all individuals will experience the same consequences (Weiss, 2019). There are several warning signs that may indicate sex addiction; however, it is important to discriminate between risky or maladaptive behaviors and sexual patterns that are merely different from the norm. The criteria that determine a sex addiction can also be used as warning signs.

While these may be fairly obvious signs that something is not right, there are other less noticeable symptoms; for example, if an individual's husband is addicted to pornography, it may not be apparent to the friends of the wife. If friends notice that the wife has become self-isolating, depressed, or angry, this may be a clue that some type of intervention is needed (American Addiction Centers, 2019b). Similarly, if friends or family notice a loved one who jumps from relationship to relationship because they cannot stand to be alone, this too may be a sign that help is needed.

Causes of Sex Addiction

There is controversy over whether or not sex addiction is real; therefore, it is difficult to say with certainty the exact causes of the disorder. Some possible factors influencing sex addiction include genes, hormones, environmental influences, existing mental health disorders, and social challenges (American Addiction Centers, 2019b).

Genes

Some individuals may have a genetic predisposition to the emotional dysregulation and/or sensory-seeking behavior that is involved in sex addiction. Additionally, research suggests that sex addiction, like with other addictive behaviors, can be partially explained through heritability. Some individuals display genetic risk factors for developing addiction, specifically with regard to substance abuse disorders (Ducci & Goldman, 2012). Similar to the ways in which food can be argued to be a substance, sex may also share substance-like qualities (Gordon et al., 2018). The extent to which genes play a role in sex addiction has not been well-studied at this time; however, research does speculate that genetics plays at least a small role in the development of addiction in general (Ducci & Goldman, 2012).

Hormones

It is possible that higher levels of hormones, such as testosterone and estrogen, can affect an individual's propensity toward sex addiction. Testosterone has been correlated to sexual functioning, but an excess of the hormone does not seem to play a critical role in libido control and sexual desires (Fong, 2006). Research suggests, however, that the reward center in the brain may be affected by sex hormones, thus enhancing the response to sexual behavior in general.

Environmental Factors

For individuals who have suffered abuse, neglect, or early exposure to sexual content, either through sexual trauma or viewing of pornographic materials, it may be more likely that they will develop an addiction to sex (American Addiction Centers, 2019b). The fast-paced and sex-centric environment of the 21st century may also feed into sexually addictive behaviors. With the increase in stress levels of those who are overworked, readily-available access to internet pornography may help in reducing feelings of anxiety in certain individuals (Mayo Clinic, 2018).

Existing Mental Health Disorders

All types of addictive behaviors, including sex addiction, have been linked to anxiety, depression, poor impulse control, and other underlying mental health disorders (Briggs et al., 2017; Hall, 2014; Rosenberg et al., 2014). Individuals suffering from bipolar disorder may be even more susceptible to sex addiction as manic states create a tendency to engage in risky or excessive behavior (American Addiction Centers, 2019b). Sex addiction can also be linked to attachment disorders in which individuals who engage in excessive sexual behaviors are really searching for feelings of secure attachment (Benfield, 2018). These individuals likely suffered neglect or abuse at an early age, experiencing feelings of insecure attachment to parents and caregivers. The use of sexual behaviors provides a temporary feeling of bonding, creating a cycle of often repetitive and risky actions (Benfield, 2018).

Social Challenges

Rejection, social isolation, and social learning are three ways in which sex addiction can be influenced by society. For individuals who are rejected in relationships and social circles, they may seek out increasingly unhealthy ways of finding sexual gratification (American Addiction Centers, 2019b). This rejection, in turn, often creates feelings of isolation within the individual. They may then experience depression from which relief is sought through the engagement of excessive or risky sex practices. Conversely, some individuals may begin their sex addiction through being part of a group; for example, if a group of men shares their extreme interest in viewing pornography, a friend who may not have engaged in this behavior before may become interested in pornography at the influence of the group. This is especially true if an individual looks up to a specific person and wants to identify with that person (American Addiction Centers, 2019b). Behaviors may quickly spiral out of control for the individual who is new to the activity.

Risk Factors for Sex Addiction

While the underlying causes of sex addiction remain uncertain, there are thought to be several risk factors for developing the disorder. As with all addiction disorders, some of these risk factors may appear in more than one type of addiction.

Biological Risk Factors

Neurobiological changes in the brain may explain an individual's propensity toward sex addiction (Phillips et al., 2015). Low levels of certain chemicals, such as dopamine or serotonin, may explain why a person develops an addiction in the first place. Individuals with family members who suffer from addiction may be more likely to develop an addiction themselves, although it is not clear if genetics can be linked to the type of addiction or simply act as an influencer (Ducci & Goldman, 2012).

For patients who suffer from frontal lobe lesions or tumors, or have seizure disorders, hypersexual behaviors have been reported (Fong, 2006). Damage to this area of the brain may result in the expression of increased sexual activity and loss of control, although this does not occur in all individuals with these conditions.

Psychological Risk Factors

Some individuals suffer from unresolved trauma which may lead to an unhealthy understanding of sex and relationships (Benfield, 2018). Professionals believe that sex addiction may be related to other mental health disorders such as obsessive-compulsive disorder, kleptomania, pyromania, pathological lying or gambling, and eating disorders such as anorexia nervosa and bulimia (Mayo Clinic, 2020). Depression, anxiety, and bipolar disorder may also play a role in the development of sex addiction (Rosenberg et al., 2014). It is important to note, however, that not all individuals with these disorders are susceptible to addictive behavior; therefore, caution must be used during assessment.

Sociocultural Risk Factors

Gender plays a role in sex addiction. More men than women have been found to be addicted to sex, although it is not uncommon for women to suffer from the same disorder (Briggs et al., 2017). Women are less likely to seek out treatment for their addiction due to the negative social connotations of having a sex addiction. Women appear to be more sensitive to the effects of stress than men, and that may help steer them into addictive patterns of behavior (Becker, McClellan, & Glover Reed, 2016).

The risk of social isolation is also a possibility for those addicted to sex and their partners (Becker et al., 2016). For the addict, isolation is a by-product of the behavior, often causing the individual to spend exorbitant time alone engaging in solo sexual behaviors or seeking out others with whom to engage sexually. Certain sexual behaviors and fantasies are socially unacceptable; therefore, the individual may choose to shy away from social situations in which they may be discovered for their inappropriate feelings and actions (Briggs et al., 2017).

Negative Effects of Sex Addiction

The effects of sex addiction are wide-ranging and depend primarily on the individual. In contrast to other addictions, sufferers may experience predominantly physical effects, although psychological and social effects are still probable. Unfortunately, the side effects of sex addiction always contribute to poor quality of life and feelings of loss of control (American Addiction Centers, 2019b):

Potential Physical and Health Impacts

- Sexually transmitted diseases and infections, such as HIV/AIDS, hepatitis B or C, or gonorrhea
- Unwanted sexual advances and harassment
- Rape
- Unwanted or unplanned pregnancy
- Physical side effects of medication to treat sex addiction including weight gain, gastrointestinal disturbances, vomiting, loss of appetite, and irritability

Potential Psychological Impacts

- Feelings of inadequacy and shame
- Anxiety/depression
- Substance abuse/misuse
- Emotional dysregulation and impulse control issues
- Symptoms that include obsessive-compulsive behaviors
- Psychological side effects of mediation to treat sex addiction including insomnia, nervousness, and headaches

Potential Social Impacts

- Social isolation (either self- or group-imposed)
- The need to hide behaviors from friends and loved ones
- Divorce or separation
- Financial impacts from spending money on sex or pornography
- Loss of job due to engaging in sexually-explicit behaviors or pornography viewing at work

The stakes are so high for someone suffering from sex addiction; therefore, it is crucial for family and friends to take notice of both the warning signs and effects, and to seek help if an addiction is suspected. Being that sex is still considered a taboo subject for many, this particular addiction can easily slip under the radar if intervention is not sought out.

Treatment for Sex Addiction

Although there appears to be more acceptance around sex addiction as a legitimate mental health disorder, some of the behaviors associated with the condition are considered morally reprehensible, and therefore difficult to discuss (Briggs et al., 2017). It is becoming more the norm that mental health professionals are learning about the treatments for sex addiction. In addition to therapeutic treatment, some individuals may benefit from medication as well. The following are some of the available treatment modalities for sex addiction (American Addiction Centers, 2019b).

Cognitive Behavioral Therapy

For individuals suffering from sex addiction, Cognitive Behavioral Therapy (CBT) focuses on identifying triggers that incite sexual behaviors and then reshaping the thoughts associated with them (Fong, 2006). If, for example, a client believes that they are not really cheating on a spouse by viewing online pornography, CBT would work to reframe this thinking to recognize the problematic behavior and underlying causes, while simultaneously working to reshape the behavior into something healthier and more positive. CBT for sex addicts also focuses on relapse prevention to ensure that the addict is in control of their behavior and not at risk to re-engage down the road (Fong, 2006).

Commercial Treatment Facilities

Residential treatment facilities offer clients a holistic healing experience, often focusing on mental, physical, and spiritual wellness. While each facility has its own focus and treatment outcomes, the majority of these facilities offer addiction treatment assistance for a wide range of addictions (American Addiction Centers, 2019b).

Couple or Marriage Counseling

This form of therapy can be beneficial for both the sex addict and their partner/spouse. Couple/marriage counseling can help to repair broken trust between couples, as well as help to improve communication skills within the relationship. Couples who participate in this form of therapy are expected to engage in reciprocal feedback while reducing partner blame. The goal is for couples to rebuild healthy behaviors, specifically with regard to sexual functioning within the relationship (American Addiction Centers, 2019b).

Dialectical Behavioral Therapy

This form of therapy is built around the idea that clients have been conditioned by the environment and peers to engage in specific behaviors (Young et al., 2019). Dialectical Behavioral Therapy (DBT) contains four specific components: skills training, individual treatment, phone coaching, and consultation. Depending on the client profile, DBT can be administered in a range of modalities (individual, group, or family). The goal of DBT is to teach mindfulness, distress tolerance, interpersonal effectiveness, and emotional regulation (Young et al. 2019).

Group Therapy

Group therapy for sex addicts is designed to provide the individual with reassurance that they are not suffering alone. The goal of group therapy is to replace negative behaviors with more positive and pro-social ones through group activities and talks designed to provide group support (American Addiction Centers, 2019b). Group therapy can be extremely beneficial for those individuals who are isolating themselves from society or fear rejection.

Individual Therapy

Individuals who choose this method of therapy can expect treatment options to focus on developing a plan to overcome sexually compulsive behaviors along with any other co-occurring disorders such as depression, anxiety, or social isolation (American Addiction Centers, 2019b). Individual therapy usually occurs in 30-60-minute sessions and can occur as frequently as the client needs. Most often, individual sessions consist of mainly talk therapy, but other options, such as neurofeedback, may be chosen if the therapist thinks it may be beneficial for the client's overall profile.

Medication

While there are currently no approved medications for the treatment of sex addiction, drugs that treat co-morbid conditions such as anxiety and depression may have a positive impact on compulsive sexual behaviors (Fong, 2006). Antidepressants can often decrease intense sexual urges, and drugs used to treat alcoholism and opioid addiction have been shown to decrease sexually compulsive behaviors. There is also a theory that anti-androgens, medications that lower sex hormones, may be useful in helping to diminish sex drive and desire; however, once these drugs are discontinued and sex hormones rise to pre-medication levels, there is a chance that the individual will return to their previous behavior (Fong, 2006).

Psychodynamic Therapy

This form of therapy is built around the idea that unconscious memories and conflicts ultimately affects an individual's behavior. Psychodynamic therapy works to uncover influencers of sex addiction that may have begun in early childhood. It is these influencers that are thought to contribute negatively to sexual patterns and behaviors. Themes commonly uncovered in psychodynamic therapy include shame, avoidance, anger, and low self-esteem and self-efficacy (Fong, 2006).

Twelve-Step Programs

For some sex addicts, 12-step programs offer similar benefits as therapy. Programs such as Sex Addicts Anonymous or Sexaholics Anonymous offer support based on the 12-step premise of Alcoholics Anonymous (American Addiction Centers, 2019b; SAA, 2020). Individuals who join these programs follow the 12 guiding principles and submit to a higher power, admitting they are powerless over their addiction (SAA, 2020). These organizations provide safety to addicts who may feel stigmatized by seeking out traditional therapeutic options. Additional organizations may have similar program structures and focus on particular methodologies such as sexual sobriety or specific groups such as LGBTQ+ (American Addiction Centers, 2019b).

Final Thoughts

While there is still a debate surrounding the validity of having a sex addiction, there is no question that excessive sexual behaviors can have a negative impact on an individual's quality of life (Briggs et al., 2017). Unfortunately, there is a scarcity of literature on truly effective evidence-based treatments for sex addiction (Delboy, 2015). For the individual and their loved ones, the struggle to maintain a normal life is daunting in the face of what is often considered a taboo condition.

If an individual is suspected of being addicted to sex, it is important for loved ones to follow the traditional channels of intervention. Seeking out treatment centers or therapists who specialize in sex addiction can be helpful in decreasing problem behavior. It is vital to realize that the sex addict is also struggling with their behavior, and that the addiction is just as much of a problem for the addict as it is for the family (Briggs et al., 2017). While this doesn't make dealing with the addiction any easier, many addicts report that they do not derive pleasure from the act of sex; rather, they feel the compulsion to participate in illicit acts to alleviate other symptoms (Briggs et al., 2017; Hall, 2014). As research develops in the field of addiction disorders, there is hope that this misunderstood condition will become easier to discuss and less complicated to treat.

Points to Remember

- *Researchers have not yet come up with answers to questions about sex addiction as a true mental health disorder.*
- *Several researchers have proposed criteria for sex addiction, but it has not yet been included in the latest edition of the DSM.*

- *There are six types of sex addicts – biological, psychological, spiritual, trauma-based, intimacy anorexic, and mood disorder-based – each has their own specific characteristics.*

- *Warning signs of sex addiction are similar to other addictions but are specific to sex and sexually-explicit behaviors.*

- *Causes of sex addiction include biological (genes, hormones), environmental, psychological, and social factors.*

- *Treatment options vary and are not specific to sex addiction, per se. Many of the treatment options can be generalized to other addiction disorders.*

Chapter 9

The Never-Ending Search for a Bargain: Understanding Shopping Addiction

Shopping can be a very polarizing pastime – people either love it or hate it. For some individuals, however, the urge to shop is all-consuming, resulting in unneeded or unwanted purchases, deep debt, and possibly bankruptcy in extreme cases (Hatfield, n.d.). Shopping addiction, or compulsive buying, is thought to occur in approximately 6% of the population (Hartston, 2012). Men and women can both be affected by this disorder, and there are no discernable differences in buying habits between genders.

As of 2019, consumer behavior has increased to an all-time high due to the explosion in online shopping options that creates an environment in which purchasing is available 24 hours a day, 7 days a week (Consumer Reports, 2019). According to Consumer Reports (2019), online sales are set to double in the next five years across the globe. In the United States alone, during 2019 e-commerce produced $435 billion in sales, which added up to a 24% increase in spending per buyer (Consumer Reports, 2019). With sales set to increase over time, it stands to reason that individuals who suffer from compulsive buying may find it more and more difficult to deal with their disorder.

For those who are afflicted by a shopping addiction, the consequences can vary. In a meta-analysis of studies on the disorder, Maraz, Griffiths, and Demotrovics (2016) revealed that of the people who suffer from compulsive buying behavior, 58.3% have large debt, 41.7% are unable to meet payments, 33.3% suffer from criticism from acquaintances, 8.3% experience legal and/or financial consequences, 8.3% experience criminal legal problems, and 45.8% experience guilt. Unfortunately, for these people, the urge to buy creates a level of anxiety that cannot be alleviated without continuing to make purchases.

Researchers have not yet determined the validity of shopping addiction (Hartston, 2012; Sohn & Choi, 2014). As of the fifth edition of the Diagnostic and Statistical Manual of Mental Disorders (American Psychiatric Association, 2013), the only close category into which shopping addiction may fit is "impulse control disorder not otherwise specified" (p. 479). Yet the symptoms felt by those who suffer from the urge to buy are very real. Moreover, the consequences suffered by those afflicted can diminish the quality of life and damage an individual's peace of mind.

Shopping Addiction: Is it Really a Disorder?

Addiction as a disorder is a delicate topic among researchers. Currently, there is only one behavioral addiction recognized in the DSM-5 (American Psychiatric Association, 2013) and that is a gambling addiction, although internet and gaming addictions have been recently considered. For a behavior such as compulsive buying, researchers have not yet been able to determine whether there is enough evidence to support its addictive nature; however, there are some indicators that suggest these types of behaviors can indeed become addicting (Hartston, 2012).

Considering these factors, compulsive buying fits into the category of addiction as most individuals who suffer from the disorder report an inability to control purchasing, the use of purchasing as an escape from negative feelings, and experiencing a rush or 'high' from the act of shopping (Cassata, 2018; Sohn & Choi, 2014). Individuals often experience behavior that is inappropriate, excessive, and disruptive; yet, they have little power to stop it even though they realize the resulting negative consequences (Maraz et al., 2016).

In 1994, McElroy and colleagues proposed a set of three diagnostic criteria for compulsive buying behavior to include

- Maladaptive preoccupation with buying or shopping or maladaptive buying or shopping impulses

- Generation of marked distress by the buying preoccupations, impulses, or behaviors, which are time-consuming, interfere significantly with social or occupational functioning or result in financial problems

- Lack of restriction of the excessive buying or shopping behavior to periods of hypomania or mania

Unfortunately, these criteria have not yet been accepted by the two major classifiers of disease, the DSM and the ICD. Researchers appear to agree that compulsive buying is a significant mental health disorder; however, they are unsure as to its origins (Granero et al., 2016).

One reason that may contribute to the lack of agreement on identifying compulsive buying as a true addiction disorder is the internet's role in influencing shopping behavior (Granero et al., 2016). Historically, shoppers needed to visit traditional brick and mortar stores in order to make purchases. Due to the age of technology, individuals only need to have access to the internet in order to shop. The internet has made buying effortless with the introduction of one-click shopping and most sites offer the ability to save credit card information for future purchases (Correa, 2020). Online shoppers also have the option of browsing through items or seeking out target items immediately without the hassle of finding them in the store (Hartston, 2012).

Online shopping is so prevalent that it may only take an individual a few minutes to search for an item, locate it, and purchase it (Correa, 2020). Items can now be delivered in one or two days, often for free. The added ease of shipping makes online shopping irresistible to some. With all of these options available, it makes sense that individuals could experience an increase in their buying behavior.

Another challenge in diagnosing shopping addiction relates to consumers' experiences in traditional stores. While internet buying is certainly on the rise, there are those individuals who prefer to shop in person. Even these environments are influenced by companies and their desire to make profits through the use of strategic marketing and a practice known as neuromarketing that uses brain research to make predictions about consumer buying patterns (Hartston, 2012).

Neuromarketing utilizes functional magnetic resonance imaging (fMRI), skin moisture level tests, breathing patterns, heart rate, and eye movement/pupil dilation to determine the effects of advertising and the likely correspondent purchasing behaviors of shoppers (Hartston, 2012). The use of the color red in advertising, for example, equates to shoppers attributing intelligence and power to the ownership of the product (Hartston, 2012). The choice of the music that is played in stores is strategically calculated to bring on a specific target emotion in the shopper, either slowing them down to browse the aisles, or creating upbeat, happy feelings that convince the consumer to purchase something from this particular store (Hartston, 2012). As a result of this targeted marketing, shoppers can be hyper-stimulated, and perhaps engage in buying practices that are different from their usual habits.

Unfortunately, there is great difficulty in parsing out whether or not it is the influences on shoppers' behavior that causes addictive-like patterns in their behavior, or if there is a physiological tendency toward shopping addiction. Although these individuals suffer from negative consequences similar to other addictions, there has not been a robust body of research supporting one theory over another (Manchiraju, Sadachar, & Ridgway, 2017). Manchiraju et al. (2017) developed a compulsive online shopping scale (COSS), based off of the Bergen Shopping Addiction Scale (Andreassen et al., 2015). These assessment tools are purported to measure specific addiction criteria as set forth in the DSM-5 (American Psychiatric Association, 2013), such as mood modification, conflict, tolerance, and withdrawal; however, more research is needed to solidify the connection between compulsive buying behavior and addiction (Andreassen et al., 2015).

Warning Signs of a Shopping Addiction

Compulsive buying appears to be an issue only in countries where individuals have disposable income and leisure time as well as locations that have a wide availability of goods (Black, 2007). There is also evidence suggesting that younger females are more susceptible to developing a compulsive shopping habit (Maraz et al., 2016). The presentation of symptoms typically appears to be late teens to early 20s, although later onset has been reported (Black, 2007). Some of the generally accepted warning signs of compulsive buying include

- *Spending more than they can afford*
- *Shopping as a reaction to feeling angry or depressed*
- *Shopping as a way to feel less guilty about a previous shopping spree*
- *Harming relationships due to spending or shopping too much*
- *Losing control of shopping*
- *Lying about how much shopping is being done or how much is being spent*
- *Hiding credit card bills, shopping bags, or receipts*
- *Borrowing money from friends and family to cover credit card bills*

  (American Addiction Centers, n.d.c, n.p.).

The type of shopping addict someone is may clue family and friends into problematic behavior. There are six proposed types of shopping addicts, each with unique behaviors related to buying and/or returning items (Addiction Hope, n.d.).

Bargain Hunters

These shoppers will purchase products that they don't need simply because they are on sale. They are driven by a need to find the cheapest or best deal in a given store. Regardless of the future use of the product, this type of shopper finds reward from spending the least money on an item (Addiction Hope, n.d.).

Bulimic Shoppers

These shoppers go through a purchase and return cycle (Addiction Hope, n.d.). They will buy multiple items in one shopping trip but then return them shortly thereafter. It is as if they want the items but are afraid of the consequences of keeping them, much like those suffering from the eating disorder.

It is important to note any of these additional behaviors as they may indicate a shopping problem. Although caution should be taken as many of the types of shoppers listed may also experience normal shopping behavior; for example, there are legitimate collectors out there who purposefully seek out additions to their collections. These people may be more likely to have a hobby than a shopping addiction.

Collectors

These individuals are interested in collected items. They will often purchase similar items in different colors, sizes, or patterns. Regardless of need, these shoppers feel as though they must have every similar item, or their collection is not complete (Addiction Hope, n.d.). They are driven by the need to collect.

Compulsion-Shopping Addicts

For these individuals, retail therapy is a way of life. They will often turn to shopping as a means of dealing with stress and other negative emotions. They may shop to avoid negative feelings or to cope with everyday stressors. The reward for these shoppers is relief from anxiety and depression (Addiction Hope, n.d.).

Flashy Shopaholics

These shoppers spend large amounts of money on the most impressive-looking purchases. The goal of this type of shopper is to impress others with their purchases (or financial prowess). The reward for the shopper is the adoration and praise of others (Addiction Hope, n.d.).

Trophy Hunters

For these shoppers, finding the perfect item drives their behavior. They are interested in finding the best of the best. They are driven by the search instead of the final purchase (Addiction Hope, n.d.).

Causes of a Shopping Addiction

There has not been much-published research into the causes of compulsive buying (Black, 2007). Some speculate that it is the result of early-life trauma, while others suggest that cultural factors influence patterns of compulsive buying (Black, 2007). There has not yet been any direct evidence supporting genetic factors as influencers of compulsive buying, although some research suggests there are cognitive distortions that inhibit buying responses in individuals with the disorder (Granero et al., 2016; Vogel et al., 2019).

For the most part, the proposed causes of compulsive buying are thought to be either psychological or cultural. For people who exhibit excessive buying patterns, it appears as though they are trying to fill an emotional void (Sohn & Choi, 2014). For facilities that treat compulsive shopping and spending, there are a wide variety of emotional challenges seen in clients. Some of the psychological conditions that are treated along with compulsive shopping include emotional deprivation in childhood, inability to tolerate negative feelings, need to fill an inner void, excitement seeking behavior, a need for perfectionism, and genuine impulsive/compulsive behaviors (The Oaks, 2018). Any of these underlying issues are what purportedly cause the individual to engage in compulsive shopping as a way to alleviate painful feelings.

As with other addictions, early-childhood trauma such as physical abuse, neglect, or sexual abuse may result in an individual developing a shopping addiction (Black, 2007). There may also be some connection to compulsive buying running in families where mood disorders and other substance abuse disorders are present. This further supports the psychological basis for compulsive buying in that individuals who see a loved one 'medicating' through purchasing may become more likely to assume this is a healthy method of dealing with negative emotions (Black, 2007).

Conversely, some research suggests that compulsive buying is caused by cultural factors related to increased internet usage and other 21st century challenges (Trotzke, Starcke, Muller, & Brand, 2015). Compulsive shopping is predominately seen in cultures where access to goods is widespread; therefore, it is difficult to say whether or not excessive shopping is the result of cultural influences such as materialism and increased wealth or if it is a true addiction (Granero et al., 2016).

With the internet so easily accessible, some individuals cannot resist the urge to shop online, which creates its own set of problems. Shopping from the comfort and privacy of home can increase the likelihood that someone who had problems with shopping behaviors in brick and mortar stores will have more intense problems with internet shopping; however, this is a new field of research in which there are no direct links supporting compulsive online shopping as its own disorder (Trotzke et al., 2015).

Risk Factors of Compulsive Shopping

As with causes, there has not been a great deal of research into the risk factors that make an individual more likely to develop compulsive shopping habits; however, there appears to be a general consensus that risk factors are likely to be either psychological or sociocultural in nature (Black, 2007; Trotzke et al.,

2015). Since shopping addiction shares similarities with other behavioral addictions, such as gambling, sex, and food, risk factors are comparable.

Psychological Risk Factors

Individuals suffering from underlying mental health disorders, such as depression, anxiety, bipolar disorder, and impulse control disorders may find that compulsive buying can act as a soothing agent for their negative feelings (Sohn & Choi, 2014). For an individual with an inability to cope with daily life stressors, shopping may provide an outlet in which they feel powerful and in control, even though the reality is that the behaviors are very much out of control.

Shopping can also be hyper-stimulating to those who suffer from low self-esteem and self-regulation. Receiving positive interactions and praise from salespeople, experiencing excitement of accomplishment from finding a deal or perfect product, or simply feeling the anticipation of the sights, smells, and sounds of visiting the mall can work to create a false sense of happiness in people who suffer from an inability to cope with stress (Hartston, 2012). Similarly, for individuals who have suffered from childhood trauma or attachment disorder, the process of shopping can function as a form of attachment (attachment to goods instead of people) from which breaking the cycle becomes overwhelmingly difficult (Hartston, 2012).

Sociocultural Risk Factors

With advertisements around every corner, on television, and popping up on social media, it is difficult to escape from the draw of consumerism. For individuals who struggle to control their shopping and spending, this overly prevalent reminder of products and services can trigger buying urges like never before (Black, 2007). The internet alone can influence individuals to shop more than they had originally intended. In 2014, online sales were estimated at $1.3 trillion globally and in 2018, they were estimated at $2.4 trillion globally (Saleh, 2018). This increase is not necessarily due to individuals discovering new products that they didn't know existed before; rather, it is due to the ease of which shopping can occur.

For individuals with compulsive buying habits, the internet functions similar to a casino for gambling addicts (American Addiction Centers, n.d.c). The promise of scoring the best deal, coupled with the ease of purchasing can be intoxicating for some. Internet shopping deals such as Cyber Monday only work to exacerbate compulsive shopping behaviors, especially for those individuals who are driven by the desire to find a deal (American Addiction Centers, n.d.c). This is especially true when the individual's friends and/or family are also participating in this form of shopping and bargain-finding.

Seeing others participate in the same behavior can encourage some individuals to normalize their compulsive actions (American Addiction Centers, n.d.c). While it is not clear if compulsive shopping can be linked to a form of internet addiction, there are signs that suggest there may be no clear line between the two (Trotzke et al., 2015).

Negative Effects of Compulsive Shopping

Unlike other addictions, compulsive shopping results in mainly psychological and sociocultural effects. Similar to other addictions, in the short term, compulsive shoppers may feel elated after completing a purchase; yet, these effects quickly wear off resulting in guilt, anxiety, and feelings of inadequacy (American Addiction Centers, n.d.c). Other negative effects of compulsive buying may include

- Major depression/mood dysregulation
- Generalized anxiety disorder
- Dishonesty
- Fear of shopping with others
- Fractured relationships with friends, spouse, or family due to financial strain
- Loss of home, car, or other personal property/bankruptcy
- Loss of job from spending too much time shopping online at work
- In extreme cases, criminal behavior such as theft or embezzlement to pay off debts
- Hoarding
  (American Addiction Centers, n.d.c; Hatfield, n.d.).

Treatment for Shopping Addiction

Many individuals with compulsive buying habits go untreated as they feel embarrassed about their behavior; however, it is important for individuals to identify what may be triggering them to excessively shop in the first place (Black, 2007). Although there has yet to be an agreement regarding shopping addiction as a disorder, there appears to be a consensus that underlying stressors contribute to the behavior (Maraz et al., 2016). Unfortunately, there are not many well-researched treatment options available specifically for shopping addiction. Most treatment options are generalized for various types of addictions and mental health disorders.

Cognitive Behavior Therapy

For some individuals suffering from compulsive buying, Cognitive Behavior Therapy (CBT) has shown promise in helping to reduce the symptoms and urges to shop, as well as to reduce the possibility of relapse (Hague, Hall, & Kellett, 2016). CBT for shopping addiction bases treatment on identifying and changing the negative thought patterns and feelings which contribute to the urge to shop (Lejoyeux & Weinstein, 2010). Within therapeutic treatment, therapists work with clients to help them learn to place value on things other than materialistic goods and the subsequent recognition that those items bring. CBT is offered in both individual and group therapy formats which may be especially helpful for those who are self-isolating due to shame over their behavior.

Commercial Treatment Programs

Most commercial treatment programs that treat shopping addiction also treat other forms of addiction. Facilities provide specialized help with spending and buying disorders such as shoplifting, overspending, hoarding, and theft (American Addiction Centers, n.d.c). These programs offer inpatient and outpatient counseling, group therapy, holistic approaches to healing, and help with relapse prevention.

Family Intervention

Another way of helping an individual reduce their compulsive behavior is through supportive intervention. Although not professional, family members can often help their loved one to reduce spending through a series of interventions such as cutting off access to cash flow, designating a family member to be in charge of finances, and not allowing the individual to go shopping alone (Tyler, 2016). It may be necessary for an individual to be monitored for necessary purchases as well, as these can quickly spiral out of control such as food, clothing, and personal products.

Medication

Studies from as far back as the 1990s suggest that treating compulsive shopping with antidepressants and opioid antagonists may help to reduce urges, therefore promoting successful outcomes for patients (Hague et al., 2016; Kim, 1998). Studies have suggested that treating compulsive shopping with anticonvulsants may be effective in altering the individual's mood, therefore alleviating the urge to shop as a way of self-medicating (Hague et al., 2016).

Twelve-Step Programs

Similar to alcohol, drug, food, sex and gambling, compulsive shoppers can find support through 12-step programs such as Debtors Anonymous and Spenders Anonymous (SA, n.d.). Both of these programs work on the 12 principles of Alcoholics Anonymous which are adapted into the landscape of compulsive buying and spending. Depending on the program, focus may be placed on abstinence from spending, or on developing plans around mindful spending. Like other 12-step programs, they are not professional in nature but provide individuals with a sort of camaraderie in which they can begin to realize they are not alone (American Addiction Centers, n.d.c).

Final Thoughts

Although shopping addiction has not yet been recognized in the DSM or ICD, researchers believe there is merit to considering it as a significant mental health disorder (Granero et al., 2016). It cannot be denied that factors associated with internet shopping have increased the availability of buying options, and this can prove detrimental for people who struggle to curb their buying urges. Increased marketing research has led to more targeted advertisements toward shoppers in the hopes of influencing buying patterns (Hartston, 2012). While more research is needed in the area of both shopping addiction and its closely-related sister disorder, compulsive online shopping, researchers do agree that individuals who exhibit patterns of compulsive buying are likely compensating for unresolved issues and/or existing mental health conditions (Black, 2007; Manchiraju et al., 2017; Maraz et al., 2016).

If an individual is suspected as having a shopping disorder, treatment options such as therapy, medication, or family intervention may provide relief from symptoms. Performing emotional wellness checks and monitoring a loved one's spending habits are critical to assessing the possibility of a shopping addiction. It is important to remember that although compulsive buying affects a relatively low percentage of the population, it can affect men and women equally.

Points to Remember

- *Shopping addiction, or compulsive buying, is thought to occur in approximately 6% of the population.*

- *Researchers have not yet determined the validity of shopping addiction.*

- *Challenges to identifying shopping addiction include the prevalence of internet shopping, as well as more sophisticated marketing research targeting certain shopper demographics.*

- *There are six types of shopping addicts – flashy shopaholics, bargain hunters, compulsion-addiction shoppers, trophy hunters, collectors, and bulimic shoppers.*

- *It is difficult to pinpoint the exact causes of shopping addiction; however, it is thought to be caused by predominately psychological and sociocultural factors*

- *Although there are treatment options available, many of these are not specific to shopping addiction and have not been well-researched.*

Chapter 10

Living in Virtual Reality: Understanding Internet and Gaming Addiction

Since its inception, the internet has provided users with a multitude of opportunities for information sharing, social networking, and entertainment (Ortiz-Ospina, 2019). With so many options at an individual's fingertips, it can be easy to get lost in the vast landscape of virtual reality. As convenient as life has become with 24/7 access to anything and everything, the internet can prove challenging to some individuals who are susceptible to the mesmerizing effects of the glowing computer screen (Cash, Rae, Steel & Winkler, 2012).

The omnipresence of the internet, along with its ease of access, has become a potential problem for some individuals, and is becoming increasingly problematic for children and adolescents (Klass, 2019). First labeled as an addiction by Goldberg in 1995, 'net addiction' as it was then called, was described as a pathology or disorder due to the overuse of technology that affected a wide range of behaviors and ability to control impulses (Goldberg, 1995, as cited in Saliceti, 2015). This disorder, also known as pathological internet use, describes a situation in which an individual cannot control their internet usage and as a result, faces social, psychological, physiological, and professional consequences (Erol & Cirak, 2019).

While there is no consensus over why some individuals become addicted to the internet, there are many theories explaining why one might be more susceptible to the addiction (Erol & Cirak, 2019; Klass, 2019; Saliceti, 2015; Tas, 2019). Age and gender are two factors that appear to have the most impact on developing an internet addiction, as young people, especially males, appear to be more likely to develop an addiction to the internet than females (Tas, 2019). Geographic location also appears to have a strong impact on internet addiction, with most addicted individuals living in Europe and North America (Tas, 2017).

While internet addiction research is still in its infancy, it can be said with some certainty that individuals who are addicted to the internet suffer from a variety of secondary mental and physical health challenges; however, understanding which came first, internet addiction or health issues, is key in providing the most effective treatment to addicted individuals (Gregory, 2019; Tas, 2019).

Internet Addiction: Is it Really a Disorder?

Internet addiction research is still in its early stages; therefore, it is difficult to say with certainty whether or not it is a legitimate disorder. Although some researchers have labeled pathological internet use as the inability of an individual to control their internet usage despite facing negative consequences, others ask if the usage of internet is less of an addiction and more of an escape from other unpleasant feelings (Arslan & Kiper, 2018; Chou et al., 2015; Erol & Cirak, 2019). It is also important to note that some researchers and organizations have created a distinction between internet addiction and gaming addiction, likely due in part to the fact that there is a scarcity of studies on general internet addiction (Tas, 2017; Zajac, Ginley, Chang, & Petry, 2017).

Once a name was given to the phenomenon of internet overuse, more research began to target the possibility that it could become a full-blown addiction. Originally described by Young (1998), five sub-types of internet addiction were identified based on the application used versus the physical act of using the internet to include

- *Cybersexual addiction: individuals are engaged in viewing, downloading and trading online pornography*

- *Cyber-relational addiction: people become overly involved in online relationship, more important than real life ones, with marital discourse and family instability (chat rooms, social networks)*

- *Net compulsion: gambling, shopping, training online*

- *Information overload: excessive web surfing and information and database search*

- *Computer addiction: individuals are overly engaged with pre-programmed games*

    (Poli, 2017, p. 5).

This research correlates with more recent studies that have suggested that users are more application-driven, which is what causes them to become addicted to the internet (Erol & Cirak, 2019; Kuss, Griffiths, & Binder, 2013; Poli, 2017). The internet is merely a medium that allows the user to access the addictive application such as social media, gaming, and relationship sites to name just a few (Erol & Cirak, 2019; Kuss et al., 2013).

During its latest revision, the DSM-5 (American Psychiatric Association, 2013), officially recognized internet gaming disorder as needing further research; however, it was proposed that it be included as a behavioral addiction. The only other such addiction recognized in the DSM-5 is gambling addiction (American Psychiatric Association, 2013). Similarly, gaming disorder will be officially recognized in the upcoming revision of the International Classification of Diseases (ICD) (American Psychiatric Association, 2018).

The DSM-5 (American Psychiatric Association, 2013) noted that gaming must cause significant impairment or distress in multiple aspects of a person's life. Although the recognition of this disorder is important, the DSM-5 (American Psychiatric Association, 2013) is specific in its classification of gaming as the problem, not general internet addiction. There is no mention of online gambling, social media, or internet pornography in the description of the disorder. The symptoms of internet gaming disorder include

- Preoccupation with gaming
- Withdrawal symptoms, such as sadness, anxiety, and irritability when the game is taken away
- The need to spend more time playing the game to satisfy the urge
- Inability, even after multiple attempts, to reduce or stop gameplay
- Giving up on other activities in favor of gameplay
- Lying to family and friends about the amount of time spent playing games
- Using gaming as a means of coping with stress or negative moods, such as guilt or hopelessness
- Risking or having lost a job due to preoccupation with gaming
- (American Psychiatric Association, 2013).

In order to fit the criteria for internet gaming disorder, the individual would have to meet at least five of the symptoms within a year (American Psychiatric Association, 2013).

Another aspect that remains unclear in the decision to classify internet addiction as a mental health disorder is whether an underlying psychological condition drives individuals toward excessive use of the internet (Poli, 2017). An individual who suffers from social anxiety, for example, may develop a propensity toward excessive internet usage as it is an outlet in which the individual can feel safe when interacting with others (Erol & Cirak, 2019; Tas & Oztosun, 2018). In this case, excessive internet usage would be a symptom of an existing disorder.

Personality, Mental Health Disorders, and the Development of Internet Addiction

Research suggests that personality traits have a direct correlation with a tendency toward internet addiction (Dong, Wang, Yang, & Zhou, 2013; Erol & Cirak, 2019). People who exhibit low emotional stability, agreeableness, and extroversion are more likely to develop excessive internet usage and individuals who exhibit impulsivity are more likely to become addicted to the internet (Dong et al., 2013; Erol & Cirak, 2019). In a study comparing impulsivity in both internet addicts and pathological gamblers, similarities were discovered suggesting that both disorders can be classified as impulse control disorders (Lee et al., 2012). Both disorders involve the individual's inability to curb urges regardless of effort, as well as a desire to continue participating, despite the outcome of negative effects.

Individuals suffering from anxiety and depression are also more likely to develop a preoccupation with the internet. Several studies have found that the existence of these underlying disorders, along with stress and other negative life factors, can significantly predict the emergence of an internet addiction (Ostovar et al., 2016; Tas, 2019; Younes et al., 2016). Low self-esteem is another predictor of excessive internet usage. University students who reported low self-esteem also reported increased insomnia, anxiety, depression, stress, and potential internet addiction (Younes et al., 2016).

An additional factor to consider in relation to increased internet usage is poor social support. Individuals who reported loneliness were more likely to spend increased time on the internet, most often seeking out social connections that otherwise eluded them in real life (Erol & Cirak, 2019). College students are especially susceptible to loneliness, as the act of being away from familial structures increases the likelihood that they will turn to the internet as a means of maintaining connection. Yet studies have shown that while increased loneliness can move an individual toward internet addiction, excessive internet use can increase loneliness and withdrawal on its own (Erol & Cirak, 2019).

Warning Signs of Internet Addiction

Although many researchers categorize internet addiction as an impulse control disorder, excessive internet usage can have a profoundly negative impact on individuals, families, and communities. As the preoccupation with the internet increases, individuals may suffer from a loss of social networks, activities and, in some cases, financial opportunities. For friends and families concerned with their loved one's internet usage, there are some commonly agreed upon warning signs that may indicate the presence of internet addiction to include

- Becoming preoccupied with the internet, or constantly thinking about past or future use

- Needing to use the internet for more time each session in order to gain satisfaction

- Making unsuccessful efforts to control, reduce, or stop the use of the internet

- Becoming restless, moody, depressed, or irritable when attempting to control internet usage

- Losing track of time while on the internet or playing an online game

- Having jeopardized a job, significant relationship, or other opportunity due to a preoccupation with the internet

- Lying to family, friends, bosses, and/or therapists about the amount of time spent on the internet

- Using the internet as a way of escaping from problems

- Becoming defensive when confronted with questions about internet usage

- Refer to their time on the internet as real-life experiences instead of recognizing that those experiences are of a virtual nature

(Greenfield, 2017; Gregory, 2019).

What is perhaps most difficult with internet addiction is that everyone is surrounded by technology - most people own smartphones, which brings the virtual world into focus with a few taps to the screen. For those suffering from internet addiction, it is virtually impossible to remove the trigger (Gregory, 2019). It is important, however, to recognize that there is a difference between internet overuse and addiction. While some people seem to check their phones constantly, some of that may be attributed to an overreliance on technology for business (Johansson, 2018). It becomes problematic when it interferes with daily life activities to the point of creating dysfunction within the individual (Greenfield, 2017; Gregory, 2019).

Causes of Internet Addiction

Just like other mental health disorders, the underlying causes are not exactly easy to pinpoint. Research suggests there are neurobiological factors, mental health vulnerabilities, and biological predispositions to developing internet addiction (Cash et al., 2012). Similar to other forms of addiction, internet usage is suggested to activate a combination of sites in the brain that affect the reward center (American Psychiatric Association, 2013). Over time, dopamine release is increased, creating a euphoric feeling when an individual engages in internet use (Cash et al., 2012). Addicted individuals associate this feeling with relaxation and stress reduction, when in reality their over-usage causes more stress on the brain by demanding a higher level of engagement to create the same feelings (American Psychiatric Association, 2013).

Similarly, some research suggests that internet addiction is a side effect of pre-existing mental health disorders such as anxiety, depression, and impulsivity (Erol & Cirak, 2019). While it is not exactly clear which came first, the internet addiction or the other mental health disorder, researchers appear to be certain that there is a strong association between excessive internet use and depression, withdrawal, hostility, interpersonal sensitivity, and anxiety (Cash et al., 2012, Erol & Cirak, 2019; Tas, 2017; Tas & Oztosun, 2018). At this time, there is not a strong body of research in this area to draw any reliable conclusions about true causation.

Another potential cause points to biological predisposition. Regarding addiction, in general, there is increasing evidence that individuals can have genetic predispositions to developing these behaviors (Cash et al., 2012). Individuals who may be predisposed to addiction do not have an adequate number of dopamine receptors in the brain, or they are lacking sufficient levels of serotonin and/or dopamine, the hormones that make an individual feel good; therefore, they have difficulty experiencing pleasure in the types of activities that others find rewarding (Cash et al., 2012). In order to gain pleasure from certain activities, individuals with addiction predisposition are more likely to engage in higher-than-average levels of participation or substance use (Cash et al., 2012). The subsequent increase in serotonin and/or dopamine allows the individual to experience pleasurable feelings but, unfortunately, they need to experience increased participation or substance use over time to maintain those feelings (Cash et al., 2012).

Recent research suggests that internet addiction might also be caused by environmental factors, specifically the ease of access to technology and the internet (Altin & Kivrak, 2018; Ortiz-Ospina, 2019). Social media applications that allow users to track family, friends, and other individuals of interest can easily become all-consuming for people as the promise of discovering new information at any time of the day or night can be exciting (Ortiz-Ospina, 2019). The variety of technological tools with which people access the internet and gaming has increased to include not just the standard desktop computer, but also tablets, notebooks, and smartphones. With virtually every store, restaurant, and coffee shop providing access to wireless internet, individuals can stay connected no matter where they are (Altin & Kivrak, 2018). Cars are now being manufactured with wireless internet to allow users to connect on the road. As of the 2017 model year, 16 vehicle brands offered in-car Wi-Fi (Popely, 2016).

With the omnipresence of both internet and technology, it is little wonder why individuals are unable to disconnect from the virtual world. As a side effect to the growth in access, children are becoming exposed to technology at younger ages. This becomes problematic, especially among school-aged children, as studies have suggested school engagement decreases as internet and gaming use increases (Tas, 2017). Children and adolescents become wrapped up in social media and gameplay, which in turn creates fewer desirable feelings about school (Tas, 2017).

Risk Factors for Internet Addiction

Although the actual diagnosis of internet addiction disorder is controversial, there are several risk factors associated with developing excessive internet usage. Internet addiction has not been as thoroughly researched as other addictive disorders partly due to the relatively recent development of the internet; therefore, researchers can only conjecture about contributing risk factors. As with other addictive disorders, however, internet addiction seems to share some similar characteristics.

Age

While internet addiction appears to affect all age categories, it is more prevalent in children, adolescents, and college-aged individuals (Erol & Cirak, 2019). Children and adolescents become preoccupied with the internet more often for gaming than for social media use, while college-aged individuals develop overuse due to social media and information seeking. In fact, college students have the highest interest in internet usage due to their desire to remain connected to family and friends, as well as to use the internet to search for information related to college work. Thus, college students develop a strong desire to become as internet literate as they can, which can lead to spending inordinate amounts of time connected to the virtual world (Erol & Cirak, 2019).

Existing Mental Health Disorders

There is a high rate of co-morbidity between excessing internet use and disorders such as depression, anxiety, and withdrawal (Cash et al., 2012; Erol & Cirak, 2019). Although it is not clear if internet addiction causes these disorders, or if there is an underlying disorder that causes the addiction, there appears to be a correlation between excessive internet usage and feelings of loneliness, social isolation, and hopelessness (Arslan & Kiper, 2018; Tas, 2017; Tas & Oztosun, 2018). An individual may be suffering from another form of addiction, such as sex addiction, in which the internet is merely used as a tool to obtain access to pornography. In this case, the internet is not the addiction, but rather a means to accessing material to satisfy another addiction (Erol & Cirak, 2019).

Poor Coping Mechanisms

Individuals who have a weak ability to cope with life stressors are more likely to find solace in the internet, especially for those who lack a strong social support network (Tas, 2019; Wu, Lee, Liao, & Cheng, 2015). The internet often provides the semblance of a social group for individuals who either do not have access to family and friends, or who have underdeveloped social skills (Erol & Cirak, 2019). An individual who uses the internet for social support, however, can often develop further negative social experiences, such as hostility toward family and friends, social anxiety, and social phobia (Gentile et al., 2011).

Situational Factors

In addition to poor coping mechanisms, situational factors such as martial conflict, experience of abuse, and job burnout can lead an individual to excessive internet usage (Saliceti, 2015). Marital conflict, for example, can often drive certain individuals to the internet in search of alternative companionship through dating websites or social chat rooms (Saliceti, 2015). Abuse victims may use the internet as a way in which to find individuals who share similar stories while maintaining anonymity. People who experience job burnout may use the internet for career-seeking options or to use social media as a means of venting frustrations. These actions are not necessarily problematic, except when they become all-consuming to the individual. Individuals who excessively use the internet as the result of situational factors are generally less likely to self-disclose their internet usage patterns to family and friends (Arslan & Kiper, 2018).

Negative Effects of Internet Addiction

The effects of internet addiction can vary depending on a variety of factors. Some individuals may experience physical symptoms, while for others, the symptoms may be psychological in nature. Research supports the idea that excessive internet usage does result in some form of negative consequence (Gregory, 2019; Wu et al., 2015).

Potential Psychological Impacts

- *Depression*
- *Dishonesty*
- *Feelings of guilt*

- *Anxiety*
- *Euphoric feelings when using the computer*
- *Inability to prioritize or keep schedules*
- *Isolation*
- *No sense of time*
- *Defensiveness*
- *Avoidance of work*
- *Agitation*
- *Mood swings*
- *Fear*
- *Loneliness*
- *Boredom with routine tasks*
- *Procrastination*

Potential Physical and Health Impacts

- *Backache*
- *Carpal Tunnel Syndrome*
- *Headaches*
- *Insomnia*
- *Poor nutrition (failing to eat or eating excessively to avoid being away from the computer)*
- *Poor personal hygiene (e.g. not bathing to stay online)*
- *Neck pain*
- *Dry eyes or other vision problems*
- *Weight gain or loss*

Potential Social Impacts

- *Financial loss (from not going to work or losing a job based on at-work internet usage)*
- *Fractured relationships (family, friends, spouses)*
- *Divorce*
- *Development of social phobias or social anxiety*
  (Gregory, 2019).

Not everyone who excessively uses the internet will experience the same symptoms; however, it is important for family and friends to monitor their loved one's internet usage if they suspect a problem. For individuals who have pre-existing mental health conditions (such as depression or bipolar disorder), the impacts of excessive internet use may be more severe (Gregory, 2019). Unfortunately, a tool has not yet been developed to diagnose internet addiction; yet, if an internet addiction is suspected, there are some commonly accepted assessment tools to help make a determination, including Young's Internet Addiction Test, the Problematic Internet Use Questionnaire (PIUQ), and the Compulsive Internet Use Scale (CIUS) (Gregory, 2019).

Treatment for Internet and Gaming Addiction

Due in part to its controversial status as a true mental health disorder, finding successful treatment options can be challenging. There is a debate over whether treatment is needed at all, as some call the disorder a "fad illness" and suggest that it can resolve on its own with self-corrective behavior and/or abstaining from the internet (Gregory, 2019). As with all addiction disorders, however, the first step is for the addict to acknowledge that there is a problem. Intervention from family and friends can also prove to be successful if the individual is willing to allow the help. While there is limited research into effective treatment options for the disorder at this time, the following are some methods that have been proposed in the existing research as showing a positive impact on curbing excessive internet use.

Therapy

Several different types of therapy have been proposed for helping individuals reduce the amount of time they spend on the internet. Perhaps the most well-known, cognitive behavioral therapy (CBT), is thought to have a positive impact on reducing the urge to use the internet. CBT works especially well if the internet addiction is based on an anxiety-related disorder, such as social anxiety or phobia (Ellis, 2019). In this case, individuals would work with their therapist on developing a plan with a goal of integrating themselves back into social situations. This is accomplished over the course of small steps, accompanied by reinforcing "homework" activities (Ellis, 2019).

In addition to CBT, dialectical behavior therapy (DBT) has also been suggested as a method of treating excessive internet use. DBT uses both classical and operant conditioning through the analysis of client behavior (Young, Mumby, & Smolinski, 2019). Therapists look at the ways in which clients have been conditioned by their environment, peer associations, etc., to behave in a certain way. Although not heavily researched in terms of treating internet addiction, DBT has shown success in treating conditions such as borderline personality disorder, suicidal ideation in both adolescent and elderly patients, and eating disorders (Young, Mumby, & Smolinski, 2019).

Various other forms of therapies have also been recommended for treating excessive internet use. Equine therapy, art therapy, and recreation/wilderness therapy have all been suggested as ways in which to treat internet addiction by relying on alternative activities to move the individual away from the internet and back into society (CRC Health, n.d.). Residential treatment centers purport to provide assistance to those struggling with internet and gaming addiction. What many of these alternative therapies have in common is that they increase the amount of physical activity for individuals who are used to a sedentary lifestyle due to their addiction (Gregory, 2019).

Medication

Some professionals suggest that medication may be helpful in treating excessive internet usage. The rationale for this comes from the fact that many individuals who are suffering from the disorder are also experiencing anxiety and depression. If those underlying conditions can be treated through medication therapy, it is possible that the internet addiction will lose its strength as the individual becomes more interested in leaving the house and having social interactions (Gregory, 2019). Ultimately, the goal of medication therapy is to increase the levels of serotonin in the brain so that individuals can rely less on external rewards to create pleasurable feelings.

Final Thoughts

Although it has not been officially classified as a mental health disorder in the psychiatric community, internet addiction is a very real condition suffered by many. Whether its origins stem from underlying mental health conditions or from environmental factors, there is no question that individuals are becoming more and more preoccupied with their devices. In 2018, more than 2,800 individuals lost their lives in distracted driving accidents (U.S. Department of Transportation, n.d.). Not all of these accidents can be attributed to the use of technology while driving; however, a good majority are the result of such behavior. Unfortunately, with technology being so accessible and with more sophisticated forms surely to be developed, these statistics will likely increase.

If an individual is suspected of having an internet or gaming addiction problem, there are options. Checking in on a loved one's internet usage, monitoring how much time they spend engaged in online tasks, and looking for accompanying signs of depression, anxiety, and social withdrawal are all helpful in getting an individual the appropriate help. While research is still ongoing, there is promise that further treatment options will become available as technology continues to advance.

Points to Remember

- *Internet addiction research is still in its infancy; therefore, it is difficult to say with certainty whether or not it is a legitimate disorder.*

- *Internet gaming disorder has been classified as needing further research, yet it has been proposed that it be included as a behavioral addiction in the next edition of the DSM.*

- *Research suggests that personality traits have a direct correlation with a tendency toward internet addiction, as do underlying mental health disorders.*

- *It is difficult to pinpoint the causes of internet addiction, although some research suggests biological predisposition, neurobiological factors, and mental health vulnerabilities as having a direct correlation with the development of internet and gaming addiction.*

- *Existing mental health disorders, age, poor coping mechanisms, and situational factors are all risk factors to developing internet addiction.*

- *Therapy and medication are both strongly-suggested treatment methods for internet addiction, although there is not yet a solid body of research to back up the effectiveness of these and other treatments.*

Part Three:
Resources

Chapter 11

Resources for Recovering Addicts, Families/Peers, and Clinicians

Coping with addiction is one of the most challenging things that an individual can face; however, supporting an addict can be equally, if not more, difficult for family and friends. While there are many clinical treatment options available for individuals suffering from addiction, it is often a complex process in trying to get those individuals the help they need. Oftentimes, addicts cannot admit that they have a problem. When they do admit the problem, they often find asking for help to be an insurmountable process. Similarly, when a family member or friend knows their loved one is suffering but feels powerless to help, it can be emotionally exhausting.

Luckily, there are many helpful resources alternative to therapy and medication for both the addicted individual and their supporters. The list of resources that follows is designed as a guide for individuals who want more information on the ways in which to cope with and treat addiction. This guide is not an exhaustive list; rather, it provides starting points for finding appropriate treatment options for both substance and behavioral addictions.

12-Step Programs

Alcoholics Anonymous (AA): AA is a non-professional, self-supporting program made up of men and women who wish to get help with a drinking problem. AA works on the premise of a 12-step program, which is a set of principles that are spiritual in nature that when practiced daily, can help to alleviate the alcoholic of their compulsion to drink. AA operates in every state in the U.S., as well as in Canada. Meetings are a key component of the program and can be attended as frequently as needed by the individual. AA also publishes a series of literature for alcoholics and their supporters. For more information, visit https://www.aa.org

Al-Anon: Al-Anon is similar to AA in that it provides support for the families and friends of alcoholics who are looking for support with their own coping skills. Working along the same lines as AA, Al-Anon offers meetings in which individuals share their feelings and experiences of living with a loved one who suffers from alcoholism. There is no cost to join Al-Anon, although members can contribute voluntarily. For teens, Al-Anon offers Alateen, which focuses on issues specific to children and teenagers coping with an alcoholic parent or loved one. For more information, visit https://al-anon.org

Clutterers Anonymous (CLA): CLA is open to anyone who has a desire to stop cluttering or hoarding and their family members. CLA follows the 12-step approach to recovery and offers meetings in 20 states. In addition to face-to-face meetings, members can participate in phone or Skype meetings. As with other 12-step programs, CLA is non-profit and relies on the donations of members to sustain its activities. For more information, visit https://clutterersanonymous.org

Debtors Anonymous (DA): DA is a 12-step program similar to AA. The program is for anyone who is a compulsive debtor (e.g. purchasing beyond their means, bouncing checks, continually paying late fees to credit card companies, etc.). DA is for individuals who have experienced adverse consequences as a result of their compulsion to spend money. Like other 12-step programs, DA works on the premise of meetings, sponsorship, and program-specific literature. For more information, visit www.debtorsanonymous.org

Food Addicts in Recovery Anonymous (FA): FA is a 12-step program based on the premise of AA. FA does not charge dues or fees, and there are no weigh-ins at meetings. FA provides a fellowship for individuals who are struggling with food addiction, encompassing overeating, undereating, obsessive dieting, restriction, and obsession with exercise. The organization welcomes individuals in all stages of recovery, and who have experienced all forms of eating disorders. Similar to other 12-step programs, FA consists of meetings and literature that is targeted to help individuals struggling with food addiction. Meetings can be found in most states. For more information, visit https://www.foodaddicts.org

Gamblers Anonymous (GA): GA is a 12-step recovery program designed to provide a fellowship treatment approach for men and women who are ready to admit they have a gambling addiction. GA does not charge membership fees, nor is the organization affiliated with any other recovery program. During the program, individuals admit they have a gambling problem and they commit to working within themselves to understand why gambling has such power. Ideally, individuals attend meetings, as often as they need, where they share their feelings with other excessive gamblers. Meetings are held in every state in the U.S. as well as internationally. Friends and supporters are welcome to attend some of the meetings, but others are reserved for excessive gamblers only. For more information, visit www.gamblersanonymous.org

Gam-Anon: For family and friends concerned about how gambling is affecting the life of a loved one, Gam-Anon provides support and resources to help individuals cope with another individual's gambling addiction. The program is similar to GA in that it follows the 12-step healing process of self-help and fellowship. Gam-Anon provides a welcoming environment in which attendees can share their experiences of living with a gambling addict. Long-time members provide additional support in the form of guidance throughout the program. For more information, visit https://www.gam-anon.org

GreySheeters Anonymous (GSA): Similar to FA in its process of sponsorship and meetings, GSA provides members with a GreySheet, which is essentially a meal plan that an individual must follow after committing to a sponsor. The food plan is based on the abstinence practice of only eating what is weighed and measured three times per day, with no snacking in between meals. These GreySheets are proprietary to the program and members can only obtain them through working with a sponsor. GSA offers meetings in most states and several countries outside of the U.S. The organization also offers phone meetings for members who cannot attend in person. For more information, visit https://www.greysheet.org

Narcotics Anonymous (NA): NA is the second-largest 12-step organization (behind AA) focused on helping individuals with drug addiction challenges. In 2018, NA catalogued approximately 70,000 meetings in 188 countries. Founded in 1953, NA is also the second-oldest 12-step recovery program (AA being founded in the 1930s). Similar to AA, members attend meetings and subscribe to the 12 principles of overcoming addiction. Although both AA and NA proclaim to be spiritual in nature, they do not subscribe to a specific religion or iteration of God. Members are encouraged to develop a relationship with a "higher power" and are to formulate their own personal understanding of that power. Another feature of both AA and NA is that they work off of sponsorship, meaning one addict helps another. These sponsors help others in learning how to follow the 12 steps and acting as a guide through the recovery process. For more information, visit https://www.na.org

Nar-Anon: Similar to Al-Anon, Nar-Anon provides support for families and friends of individuals struggling with drug addiction. Nar-Anon offers meetings and support groups in which families and friends can share their feelings with others who have had similar experiences. Nar-Anon is not for addicts themselves, but rather offers a safe space for their family and friends to apply the 12-step program as a means of developing increased coping skills. For more information, visit https://www.nar-anon-org

Overeaters Anonymous (OA): Another 12-step program for overcoming food addiction, OA offers members a support system of shared experiences around food and its power to make life unmanageable for some individuals. Similar to FA, OA invites individuals suffering from a variety of eating disorders who feel their lives are out of control around food. OA is not affiliated with any other public or private organization, political movement, or religious doctrine, although they do share the 12-step process with other such programs. OA offers literature and podcasts to help new and existing members stick with the program. For more information, visit https://oa.org

Sex Addicts Anonymous (SAA): SAA's purpose is to help stop addictive sexual behavior and to help others recover from sexual addiction. The organization encourages members to admit they are powerless of their sexual addiction and are incapable of changing without help from someone or something outside of oneself. Through a 12-step process with meetings and sponsorship, SAA aims to provide members with freedom from sexual addiction. Members are only required to have a desire to stop sex addiction. For more information, visit https://saa-recovery.org

Various Drug-Related 12-Step Programs: Similar to AA and NA, there are several other 12-step recovery programs specific to the type of drug. Cocaine Anonymous, Crystal Meth Anonymous, and Heroin Anonymous are all examples of 12-step, meeting-based, non-profit programs that operate on a similar premise to AA and NA. In these programs, participants work on applying the 12 principles to their lives and utilize the help of sponsors to guide them through the recovery process. For more information on these programs, visit https://ca.org (Cocaine Anonymous), https://crystalmeth.org (Crystal Meth Anonymous), or https://heroinanonymous.org (Heroin Anonymous)

Other Resources

American Academy of Addiction Psychiatry (AAAP): The AAAP provides a member-supported resource of medical professionals, mental health practitioners, educational faculty, and other related professionals who are committed to advancing research and evidence-based practices in the field of addictive disorders. This resource offers information into the latest research surrounding addiction and the promotion of prevention and treatment options for addicts at every step in the recovery process. For more information, visit https://www.aaap.org

American Addiction Centers (AAC): AAC provides site-based treatment options for families and individuals suffering from a myriad of behavioral addictions. They provide intervention services to help families and friends get the individual into treatment, as well as providing targeted treatment services to help the individual overcome their compulsion. In addition to providing support for substance abuse addictions, AAC offers help with sex/love addiction, shopping addiction, gambling addiction, internet addiction, exercise addiction, and food addiction. AAC has locations in California, Florida, Massachusetts, Rhode Island, Mississippi, Nevada, New Jersey, and Texas. For more information, visit https://americanaddictioncenters.org/behavioral-addictions

American Association for Sex Addiction Therapy (AASAT): Geared toward the therapist looking to learn more about working with sex addicts, AASAT offers literature and training options in sex addiction, partners recovery, and intimacy anorexia. The president of AASAT, Dr. Doug Weiss, offers a separate resource via https://sexaddict.com which offers additional support for sex addiction, pornography addiction, and treatment options. On this website, individuals can discover more information about the six types of sex addicts, as well as discover if they fit the criteria of having a sex addiction. For more information on AASAT, visit https://aasat.org

Learn to Cope (LTC): Founded in 2004, LTC is a non-profit peer-led support network with 25 chapters throughout Massachusetts, two chapters in Florida, and one chapter in Idaho. LTC was founded by Joanne Peterson, who discovered her own son had developed an opioid addiction. Driven to help other families experiencing similar hardships, Peterson designed LTC to provide support, education, and resources in the hopes of benefitting others. LTC holds events and meetings that focus on addiction, recovery, and the

stigma surrounding an addiction diagnosis. For more information, visit
https://www.learn2cope.org

National Council on Problem Gambling (NCPG): The NCPG is a member-supported organization whose mission is to serve as the national advocate for programs and services in order to help individuals and families affected by excessive gambling. Their aim is to improve the health and wellness of individuals suffering from gambling addiction by helping to reduce the personal, social, and economic costs of the disorder. Founded in 1972, NCPG has remained neutral on the position of legalized gambling and serves to solely represent those who are affected by problem gambling. NCPG provides resources for learning how to responsibly gamble, as well as advocacy initiatives to bring the disorder into mainstream consciousness. For more information, visit https://www.ncpgambling.org

RISE Gaming Recovery: Located in California, RISE Gaming Recovery was designed to treat the ever-growing epidemic of obsessive gaming and its effects on young people. RISE is a residential treatment center in which patients live on the premises and participate in such activities as workshops, individual and group counseling, and diverse physical experiences such as rock climbing, surfing, and visits to area theme parks. Participants must be at least 18 years of age and be willing to live on campus as a residential guest of the facility. The program is two months in length and is not covered by insurance at this time. For more information, visit https://www.risegamingrecovery.com

SMART Recovery: As part of its mission, SMART Recovery aims to help people achieve independence from addiction problems using a scientifically-based four-point program. Created as a non-profit abstinence program, SMART Recovery does not use labels such as addict or alcoholic, but rather focuses on long-term change through the creation of a positive lifestyle. The program teaches healthy coping skills as replacements for the destructive patterns of addiction. Their four-point program focuses on building and maintaining the motivation to change, understanding and coping with the urges to engage in addictive behaviors, managing thoughts and feelings without engaging in addictive behaviors, and living and maintaining a healthy, balanced life. SMART Recovery has sites in New England, the Midwest, Florida, and the southeastern United States, as well as internationally in Canada, Australia, and parts of Europe and Africa. For more information, visit https:// www.smartrecovery.org

Substance Abuse and Mental Health Services Administration (SAMHSA): SAMHSA is an agency within the United States Department of Health and Human Services that helps to lead efforts in increasing behavioral health throughout the country. Their goal is to reduce the impact of substance abuse and mental health on American communities. The agency provides a number of resources, including assisting individuals and their families in finding treatment for both substance abuse and mental illness, providing suicide prevention support lines, and offering practitioner training in treating substance abuse and mental health disorders. SAMHSA also focuses on recovery support for military veterans who are dealing with PTSD and the effects that go along with the disorder. For more information, visit https://www.samhsa.gov

The Center for Internet and Technology Addiction: Founded by Dr. David Greenfield, an Assistant Clinical Professor of Psychiatry at the University of Connecticut School of Medicine, the Center for Internet and Technology Addiction focuses on providing resources for individuals and families struggling with the presence of internet addiction. Offerings on the Center's website include access to a virtual library of new stories, book excerpts and more dealing with internet addiction, stories from real-life individuals who have struggled with or been impacted by internet addiction, and a selection of videos from the Center's founder, lecturing on a variety of technology addiction topics. In addition to the resources available on the website, Dr. Greenfield offers personal and business consultations and presentations on internet and technology addiction. For more information, visit https://virtual-addiction.com

The Hazelden Betty Ford Foundation: Perhaps one of the most well-known foundations for the treatment of substance abuse, the Hazelden Betty Ford Foundation is the largest non-profit treatment provider, which includes 17 treatment sites throughout the United States. The foundation provides prevention and recovery options for both youth and adults. In addition to providing treatment services, the Hazelden Betty Ford Foundation offers educational opportunities in addiction studies, and is at the forefront of research in the areas of addiction and substance abuse. As an additional offering, friends and families are provided with information on the ways in which to support recovering addicts, as well as how to best choose a treatment model and facility. For more information, visit https://www.hazeldenbettyford.org

Zur Institute: The Zur Institute offers a selection of online courses on the ways in which to assess and treat internet addiction disorder. They also offer several general online resources for internet addiction, including self-tests, treatment options, internet safety information, and help for parents. Although geared toward providing continuing education to psychotherapists and other health care workers, the Zur Institute offers resources that are accessible to individuals who are not in the health care field. For more information, visit https://www.zurinstitute.com

References

Abbott, M., Binde, P., Clark, L., Hodgins, D., Johnson, M., Manitowabi, D., ... & Williams, R. (2018). *Conceptual framework of harmful gambling: An international collaboration* (3rd ed.). Gambling Research Exchange Ontario (GREO), Guelph, Ontario, Canada. DOI: 10/33684/CFHG3.en

Addiction Center. (n.d.). *Cognitive behavioral therapy.* Retrieved from https://www.addictioncenter.com/treatment/cognitive-behavioral-therapy/

Addiction Hope. (n.d.). Exploring the different types of shopping addictions that can weigh you down. Retrieved from https://www.addictionhope.com/blog/types-of-shopping-addictions-weigh-you-down/

Alaska Division of Behavioral Health. (2011). *Risk and protective factors for adolescent substance abuse.* Retrieved from http://dhss.alaska.gov/dbh/Documents/Prevention/programs/spfsig/pdfs/Risk_Protective_Factors.pdf

Alavi, S.S., Ferdosi, M., Jannatifard, F., Eslami, M., Alaghemandan, H., & Setare, M. (2012).

Behavioral addiction versus substance addiction: Correspondenve of psychiatric and psychological views. *International Journal of Preventive Medicine, 3*(4), 290-294. Retrieved from https://www.ncbi.nlm.nih.gov/pmc/articles/PMC3354400/

Alcohol and Drug Foundation. (2019). *Heroin.* Retrieved from https://adf.org.au/drug-facts/heroin/

Alcoholics Anonymous World Services, Inc. (2020). *What is AA?* Retrieved from https://www.aa.org/pages/en_US/what-is-aa

Altin, M. & Kivrak, A.O. (2018). The social media addiction among Turkish university students. *Journal of Education and Training Studies, 6*(12). DOI: 10.11114/jets.v6i12.3452

American Addiction Centers. (2019a). *Cognitive behavioral therapy techniques and addiction treatment.* Retrieved from https://americanaddictioncenters.org/cognitive-behavioral-therapy

American Addiction Centers. (2019b). Sex addiction symptoms, causes, and effects. Retrieved from https://www.psychguides.com/behavioral-disorders/sex-addiction/

American Addiction Centers. (2020a). *Cocaine abuse signs.* Retrieved from https://americanaddictioncenters.org/cocaine-treatment/signs

American Addiction Centers. (2020b). *Length of stay at a sober living home.* Retrieved from https://americanaddictioncenters.org/sober-living/length-of-stay

American Addiction Centers. (n.d.a). *Inpatient drug addiction treatment.* Retrieved from https://drugabuse.com/?s=inpatient+treatment

American Addiction Centers. (n.d.b). *Eating disorder symptoms, causes and effects.* Retrieved from https://www.psychguides.com/eating-disorder/symptoms-causes-and-effects/

American Addiction Centers. (n.d.c). Shopping addiction: Symptoms, causes and effects. Retrieved from https://www.psychguides.com/behavioral-disorders/shopping-addiction/

American Psychiatric Association. (1980). *Diagnostic and statistical manual of mental disorders.* (3rd ed.). American Psychiatric Association: Washington, DC.

American Psychiatric Association. (1994). *Diagnostic and statistical manual of mental disorders.* (4th ed.). American Psychiatric Association: Washington, DC.

American Psychiatric Association. (2013). *Diagnostic and statistical manual of mental disorders* (5th ed.). Arlington, VA: APA Publishing.

American Psychiatric Association. (2017). *What is addiction?* Retrieved from https://www.psychiatry.org/patients-families/addiction/what-is-addiction

American Psychiatric Association. (2018). Internet gaming. Retrieved from https://www.psychiatry.org/patients-families/internet-gaming

American Psychological Association. (2017). Age of first exposure to pornography shapes men's attitudes toward women. Retrieved from https://www.apa.org/news/press/releases/2017/08/pornography-exposure

American Psychological Association. (n.d.a). *What is cognitive behavioral therapy?* Retrieved from https://www.apa.org/ptsd-guideline/patients-and-families/cognitive-behavioral

American Psychological Association. (n.d.b). *What is exposure therapy?* Retrieved from https://www.apa.org/ptsd-guideline/patients-and-families/exposure-therapy

American Psychological Association. (n.d.c). *Addiction.* Retrieved from https://www.apa.org/topics/addiction/

Anderson, P. (2014). *Updated 'tool kit' to prevent opioid overdose.* Retrieved from https://www.medscape.com/viewarticle/831318

Andreassen, C.S., Griffiths, M.D., Pallesen, S., Bilder R.M., Torsheim, T., & Aboujoude, E. (2015). The Bergen shopping addiction scale: Reliability and validity of a brief screening test. *Frontiers in Psychology, 6,* 1374. DOI: 10.3389/fpsyg/2015.01374

Anthony, A. (2018). *Sexual addiction, desire and dopamine hits.* Retrieved from https://www.theguardian.com/global/2018/apr/22/sexual-addiction-desire-and-dopamine-hits

Arslan, N. & Kiper, A. (2018). Self-disclosure and internet addiction. *Malaysian Online Journal of Educational Technology, 6*(1), 56-63. Retrieved from https://files.eric.ed.gov/fulltext/EJ1165449.pdf

Bakhshani, N. (2014). Impulsivity: A predisposition toward risky behaviors. *International Journal of High Risk Behaviors & Addictions, 3*(2), e20428. DOI: 10.5812/ijhrba.20428

Becker, J.B., McClellan, M., & Glover Reed, B. (2016). Sociocultural context for sex differences in addiction. *Addiction Biology, 21*(5), 1052-1059. DOI: 10.111/adb.12383

Benfield, J. (2018). Secure attachment: An antidote to sex addiction? A thematic analysis of therapists' experiences of utilizing attachment-informed treatment strategies to address sexual compulsivity. *Sexual Addiction and Compulsivity, 25*(1), 12-27. DOI: 10.1080/10720162.2018.1462746

Berenson, A.B., Laz, T.H., Pohlmeier, A.M., Rahman, M., & Cunningham, K.A. (2015). Prevalence of food addiction among low-income reproductive-aged women. *Journal of Women's Health, 24*(9), 740-744. DOI: 10.1089/jwh. 2014.5182

Black, D. (2007). A review of compulsive buying disorder. *World Psychiatry: Official Journal of the World Psychiatric Association, 6*(1), 14-18. Retrieved from https://www.ncbi.nlm.nih.gov/pmc/articles/PMC1805733/

Bose, J., Hedden, S.L., Lipari, R.N. & Park-Lee, E. (2018). Key substance use and mental health indicators in the United States: Results from the 2017 national survey on drug use and health (HHS Publication no. SMA 18-5068, NSDUH series H-53). *Center for Behavioral Health Statistics and Quality, Substance Abuse and Mental Health Services Administration.* Retrieved from https:// www.samhsa.gov/data/sites/default/files/cbhsq-reports/NSDUHFFR2017/ NSDUHFFR2017.pdf

Brande, L. (2017). *Alcohol overdose.* Retrieved from https://drugabuse.com/ alcohol-overdose/

Brevers, D., & Noël, X (2013). Pathological gambling and the loss of willpower: A neurocognitive perspective. *Socioaffective Neuroscience & Pathology, 3*(1), DOI: 10.3402/snp.v3i0.21592

Briggs, J., Gough, B., & das Nair, R. (2017). Losing control in sex addiction: "Addict" and "non-addict" accounts. *Sexual and Relationship Therapy, 32*(2), 195-209. DOI: 10.1080/14681994.2016.1276551

Bullen, C., Verbiest, M., Galea-Singer, S., Kurdziel, T., Laking, G., Newcombe, D., Parag, V., & Walker, N. (2018). The effectiveness and safety of combining varenicline with nicotine e-cigarettes for smoking cessation in people with mental illnesses and addictions: study protocol for a randomised-controlled trial. *BMC Public Health, 18*(1), 596. https://doi.org/10.1186/s12889-018-5351-7

Business News Daily. (2020). *Why sex sells...more than ever.* Retrieved from https://www.businessnewsdaily.com/2649-sex-sells-more.html

Carlisle, K.L., Buser, J.K., & Carlisle, R.M. (2012). Childhood food addiction and the family. *The Family Journal: Counseling and Therapy for Couples and Families, 20*(3), 332-339. DOI: 10.1177/1066480712449606

Carnes, P.J., Green, B.A., Merlo, L.J., Polles, A., Carnes, S., & Gold, M.J. (2012). PATHOS: A brief screeing application for assessing sexual addiction. *Journal of Addiction Medicine 6*(1), 29-34. DOI: 10.1097/ADM.0b013e3182251a28

Cash, H., Rae, C.D., Steel, A.H. & Winkler, A. (2012). Internet addiction: A brief summary of research and practice. *Current Psychiatry Review, 8*(4), 292-298. DOI: 10.2174/157340012803520513

Cassata, C. (2018). The 7 warning signs of shopping addiction. Retrieved from https://psychcentral.com/blog/the-7-warning-signs-of-shopping-addiction/

Centers for Disease Control and Prevention. (2011). *Morbidity and mortality weekly report (MMWR).* Retrieved from https://www.cdc.gov/mmwr/ preview/mmwrhtml/mm6044a2.htm?s_cid=mm6044a2_w

Centers for Disease Control and Prevention. (2017). *Opioid overdose: Prescription opioids.* Retrieved from https://www.cdc.gov/drugoverdose/opioids/prescribed.html

Centers for Disease Control and Prevention. (2018a). *Alcohol and public health: Frequently asked questions.* Retrieved from https://www.cdc.gov/alcohol/faqs.htm

Centers for Disease Control and Prevention. (2018b). *Learn about nicotine replacement therapy.* Retrieved from https://www.cdc.gov/tobacco/campaign/tips/quit-smoking/guide/explore-medications.html

Centers for Disease Control and Prevention. (2018c). *Understanding the epidemic.* Retrieved from https://www.cdc.gov/drugoverdose/epidemic/index.html

Centers for Disease Control and Prevention. (2019a). *Opioid Overdose.* Retrieved from https://www.cdc.gov/drugoverdose/index.html

Centers for Disease Control and Prevention. (2019b). *Smoking & tobacco use.* Retrieved from https://www.cdc.gov/tobacco/data_statistics/fact_sheets/fast_facts/index.htm

Centers for Disease Control and Prevention. (2019c). *Heroin overdose.* Retrieved from www.cdc.gov/drugoverdose/data/heroin.html

Centers for Disease Control and Prevention. (2019d). *Opioid Overdose: Other drugs.* Retrieved from https://www.cdc.gov/drugoverdose/data/otherdrugs.html

Cherry, K. (2019). *An overview of stimulants and how they're used.* Retrieved from https://www.verywellmind.com/what-are-stimulants-2795573

Choliz, M. (2016). The challenge of online gambling: The effect of legalization on the increase in online gambling addiction. *Journal of Gambling Studies, 32,* 749-756. DOI: 10.1007/s10899-015-9558-6

Chou, W.P., Ko, C.H., Kaufman, E.A., Crowell, S.E., Hsiao, R.C., Wang, P.W., Lin, J.J., & Yen, C.F. (2015). Association of stress coping strategies with internet addiction in college students: The moderating effect of depression. *Comprehensive Psychiatry, 62,* 27-33. DOI: 10.1016/j.comppsych.2015.06.004

Compton, W.M., Han, B., Blanco, C., Johnson, K. & Jones, C.M. (2018). Prescription stimulant use, misuse, use disorders, and motivations for misuse among adults in the United States. *The American Journal of Psychiatry.* https://doi.org/10.1176/appi.ajp.2018.1701048

Consumer Report. (2019). Total consumer report 2019. Retrieved from https://www.nielsen.com/us/en/insights/report/2019/total-consumer-report-2019/

Correa, G. (2020). *Shopping addiction fueled by online shopping.* Retrieved from https://www.addictioncenter.com/news/2020/01/shopping-addiction-online-shopping/

CRC Health. (n.d.). *What is equine therapy?* Retrieved from https://www.crchealth.com/types-of-therapy/what-is-equine-therapy/

Crockford, D.N., Goodyear, B., Edwards, J., Quickfall, J. & el-Guebaly, N. (2005). Cue-induced brain activity in pathological gamblers. *Biological Psychiatry, 58*(10), 787-795. DOI: 10.1016/j.biopsych.2005.04.037

Davis, K. (2018). *Anabolic steroids: What you should know.* Retrieved from https://www.medicalnewstoday.com/articles/246373.php

Delboy, S. (2015). Evidence-based practice for sex addiction: A clinical case illustration. *Sexual Addiction and Compulsivity, 22*(4), 273-289. DOI: 10.1080/10720162.2015.1072487

Dodgson, L. (2017). *Sex addiction might not be a real condition – here's why.* Retrieved from https://www.businessinsider.com/experts-disagree-whether -sex-addiction-is-real-2017-10

Dong, G., Wang, J., Yang, X., & Zhou, H. (2013). Risk personality traits of internet addiction: A longitudinal study of internet-addicted Chinese university students. *Asia-Pacific Psychiatry, 5*(4), 316-321. DOI: 10.1111/j.1758-5872. 2012.00185.x

Ducci, F. & Goldman, D. (2012). The genetic basis of addictive disorders. *Psychiatric Clinics of North America 35*(2), 495-519. DOI: 10.1016/j.psc. 2012.03.010

Ellis, L.D. (2019). What is cognitive behavioral therapy (CBT)? Exploring the concept and its benefits. Retrieved from https://www.psycom.net/what-is-cognitive-behavioral-therapy-cbt

Erol, O. & Cirak, N.S. (2019). Exploring the loneliness and internet addiction level of college students based on demographic variables. *Contemporary Educational Technology, 10*(2), 156-172. DOI: 10.30935/cet.554488

Fauth-Bühler, M., Mann, K., & Potenza, M.N. (2016). Pathological gambling: A review of the neurobiological evidence relevant for its classification as an addictive disorder. *Addiction Biology, 22*(4), 885-897. DOI: 10.1111/adb.12378

FDA. (2018). *FDA approves the first non-opioid treatment for management of opioid withdrawal symptoms in adults.* Retrieved from https://www.fda.gov/ news-events/press-announcements/fda-approves-first-non-opioid-treatment-management-opioid-withdrawal-symptoms-adults

FDA. (2017). *FDA grants marketing authorization of the first device for use in helping to reduce the symptoms of opioid withdrawal.* Retrieved from https:// www.fda.gov/news-events/press-announcements/fda-grants-marketing-authorization-first-device-use-helping-reduce-symptoms-opioid-withdrawal

Felman, A. (2018). *Everything you need to know about nicotine.* Retrieved from https://www.medicalnewstoday.com/articles/240820.php

Figee, M., Pattij, T., Willuhn, I., Luigjes, J., van den Brink, W., Goudriaan, A., ... & Denys, D. (2016). Compulsivity in obsessive-compulsive disorder and addictions. *European Neuropsychopharmacology, 26*(5), 856-868. DOI: 10.1016/ j.euroneuro.2015.12.003

Fleming, R. (2015). Does alcohol damage the adolescent brain? Neuroanatomical and neuropsychological consequences of adolescent drinking. *Neuroscience and Neuroeconomics, 4,* 51-60. DOI: 10.2147/ NAN.S60983

Flint, A.J., Gearhardt, A.N., Corbin, W.R., Brownell, K.D., Field, A.E., & Rimm, E.B. (2014).

Food addiction scale measurement in 2 cohorts of middle-aged and older women. *American Journal of Clinical Nutrition, 99*(3), 578-586. DOI: 10.3945/ajcn.113.068965

Florence, C.S., Zhou, C., Luo, F., Xu. L. (2016). The economic burden of prescription opioid overdose, abuse, and dependence in the United States, 2013. *Medical Care, 54*(10), 901-906. DOI: 10.1097/MLR.0000000000000625

Fong, T.W. (2005). The biopsychosocial consequences of pathological gambling. *Psychiatry (Edgmont), 2*(3), 22-30. Retrieved from https://www.ncbi.nlm.nih.gov/pmc/articles/PMC3004711/

Fong, T.W. (2006). Understanding and managing compulsive sexual behaviors. *Psychiatry, 3*(11), 51-58. Retrieved from https://www.ncbi.nlm.nih.gov/pmc/articles/PMC2945841/

Food Addicts Anonymous. (n.d.). Abstinence. Retrieved from https://www.foodaddictsanonymous.org/abstinence

Fowler, J.S., Wolkow, N.D., Kassed, C.A. & Chang, L. (2007). Imaging the addicted brain. *Science & Practice Perspectives, 3*(2), 4-16. DOI: 10.1151/spp07324

Frayn, M., Sears, C.R., & von Ranson, K.M. (2016). A sad mood increases attention to unhealthy food images in women with food addiction. *Appetite, 100,* 55-63. DOI: 10.1016/j.appet.2016.02.008

Freedman, N.D., Schatzin, A., Leitzmann, M.F., Hollenbeck, A.R. & Abnet, C.C. (2007). Alcohol and head and neck cancer risk in a prospective study. *British Journal of Cancer, 96*(9), 1469-1474. DOI: 10.1038/sj.bjc.6603713

Galbicsek, C. (2019). *Alcohol withdrawal.* Retrieved from https://www.alcoholrehabguide.org/alcohol/withdrawal/

Gearhardt, A.N., Corbin, W.R., & Brownell, K.D. (2009). Preliminary validation of the Yale Food Addiction Scale. *Appetite, 52*(2), 430-436. DOI: 10.1016/j.appet.2008.12.003

Gearhardt, A.N., Yokum, S., Orr, P.T., Stice, E., Corbin, W.R., & Brownell, K.D. (2011). Neural correlates of food addiction. *Archives of General Psychiatry, 68*(8), 808-816. DOI: 10.1001/archgenpsychiatry.2011.32

Gentile, D.A., Choo, H., Liau, A., Sim, T., Li, D., Fung, D. & Khoo, A. (2011). Pathological video game use among youths: A two-year longitudinal study. *Pediatrics, 127*(2), e319-e329. DOI: 10.1542/peds.2010-1353

Gonsalves, Antone (2007, April 2). Report Documents Video Game Addiction. *Information Week* [online]. Retrieved from http://www.informationweek.com/news/internet/showArticle.jhtml?articleID=1987019 37

Goodman A. (1997). Sexual addiction: diagnosis, etiology, and treatment. In: J.H. Lowinson, P. Ruiz, R.B. Millman, J.G. Langrod (eds), *Substance Abuse: A Comprehensive Textbook* (3rd ed.), pp. 340-354. Baltimore: Williams & Wilkins

Gordon, E.L., Ariel-Donges, A.H., Bauman, V., & Merlo, L.J. (2018). What is the evidence for "food addiction?" A systematic review. *Nutrients, 10*(4), 477-507. DOI: 10.3390/nu10040477

Gorla, K., & Mathews, M. (2005). Pharmacological treatment of eating disorders. *Psychiatry, 2*(6), 43-48. Retrieved from https://www.ncbi.nlm.nih.gov/pmc/articles/PMC3000192/

Goudriaan, A.E., de Ruiter, M.B., van der Brink, W., Oosterlaan, J. & Vetlman, D.J. (2010). Brain activation patterns associated with cur reactivity and craving in abstinent problem gamblers, heavy smokers and healthy controls: An fMRI study. *Addiction Biology, 15*(4), 491-503. DOI: 10.1111/j.1369-1600.2010. 00242.x

Gough, C. (2019). *Revenue from fantasy sports in the United States 2018, by segment.* Retrieved from https://www.statista.com/statistics/820972/ revenue-fantasy-sports-segment/

Granero, R., Fernandez-Aranda, F., Mestre-Back, G., Steward, T., Bano, M., del Pino-Gutierrez, A., ... & Jimenez-Murcia, S. (2016). Compulsive buying behavior: Clinical comparison with other behavioral addictions. *Frontiers in Psychology, 15*(7), 914. DOI: 10.3389/fpsyg.2016.00914

Grant, J.E., Atmaca. M., Fineberg, N.A., Fontenelle, L.F., Matsunaga, H., Reddy ...& Stein, D.J. (2014). Impulse control disorders and "behavioural addictions" in the ICD-11. *World Psychiatry, 13*(2). DOI 10.1002/wps.20115

Greenfield, D. (2017). The center for internet and technology addiction. Retrieved from https://virtual-addiction.com

Gregory, C. (2019). *Internet addiction disorder.* Retrieved from https://www. psycom.net/iadcriteria.html

Guarnotta, E. (2018). *Benzodiazepine overdose: Know the signs.* Retrieved from https://drugabuse.com/benzodiazepines/overdose/

Gunnars, K. (2019a). 8 common symptoms of food addiction. Retrieved from https://www.healthline.com/nutrition/8-symptoms-of-food-addiction#section4

Gunnars, K. (2019b). Top 4 treatment options for food addiction. Retrieved from https://www.healthline.com/nutrition/food-addiction-treatment-find -help

Hague, B., Hall, J., & Kellett, S. (2016). Treatments for compulsive buying: A systematic review of the quality, effectiveness, and progression of the outcome evidence. *Journal of Behavioral Addictions, 5*(3), 379-394. DOI: 10.1556/2006.5.2016.064

Hales, C.M., Carroll, M.D., Fryar, C.D. & Ogden, C.L. (2020). Prevalence of obesity and severe obesity among adults: United States 2017-2018. Retrieved from https://www.cdc.gov/nchs/data/databriefs/db360-h.pdf

Hales, S., Blackwell, S.E., Di Simplicio, M., Iyadurai, L., Young, K., & Holmes, E.A. (2015). Assessment in cognitive therapy. In G.P. Brown & D.A. Clark (eds). *Imagery-Based Cognitive-Behavioral Assessment.* New York: Guilford Press. https://www.ncbi.nlm.nih.gov/books/NBK311390/

Hall, P. (2014). Sex addiction - an extraordinarily contentious problem. *Sexual and Relationship Therapy, 29*(1), 68-75. DOI: 10.1080/14681994.2013.861898

Hartston, H. (2012). The case for compulsive shopping as an addiction. *Journal of Psychoactive Drugs, 44*(1), 64-67. DOI: 10.1080/02791072.2012.660110

Harvard Health Publishing. (2011). *Addiction hijacks the brain.* Retrieved from https://www.health.harvard.edu/newsletter_article/how-addiction-hijacks-the-brain

Harvard Medical School. (2019). *Alcohol withdrawal: What is it?* Retrieved from https://www.health.harvard.edu/a_to_z/alcohol-withdrawal-a-to-z

Hatfield, R.C. (2019). *What are hallucinogens?* Retrieved from https://drugabuse.com/what-are-hallucinogens/

Hatfield, H. (n.d.). *Shopping spree, or addiction?* Retrieved from https://www.webmd.com/mental-health/addiction/features/shopping-spree-addiction#1

Heshmat, S. (2018). *5 patterns of compulsive buying: How do you know if you have an addiction?* Retrieved from https://www.psychologytoday.com/us/blog/science-choice/201806/5-patterns-compulsive-buying

Hiller-Sturmhofel, S. & Swartzwelder, H.S. (n.d.). *Alcohol's effects on the adolescent brain-What can be learned from animal models.* Retrieved from https://pubs.niaaa.nih.gov/publications/arh284/213-221.htm

Hilliard, J. (2019). *Central nervous system depressants.* Retrieved from https://www.addictioncenter.com/drugs/drug-classifications/central-nervous-system-depressants/

Iliades, C. (March 22, 2016). *8 common behavioral addictions.* Retrieved from https://www.everydayhealth.com/addiction-pictures/the-8-most-surprising-addictions.aspx

Jazaeri, S.A. & Bin Habil, M.H. (2012). Reviewing two types of addiction – Pathological gambling and substance abuse. *Indian Journal of Psychological Medicine, 34*(1), 5-11. DOI: 10.4103/0253-7176.96147

Jesse, S., Brathen, G., Ferrara, M., Keindl, M., Ben-Menachem, E., Tanasescu, R., Brodtkorb, E., Hillbom, M., Leone, M.A., & Ludolph, A.C. (2016). Alcohol withdrawal syndrome: Mechanisms, manifestations, and management. *Acta Neurologica Scandinavica, 135*(1). DOI: 10.1111/ane.12671

Jha, P., Chaloupka, F.J., Moore, J., Gajalakshmi, V., Gupta, P.C., Peck, R., Asma, S. & Zatonski, W. (2006). Tobacco addiction. In D.T. Jamison, J.G. Breman, A.R. Measham, G. Alleyne, M. Claeson, D.B. Evans, P. Jha, A. Mills, & P. Musgrove, *Disease Control Priorities in Developing Countries* (2nd ed.), pp. 851-868. New York, Oxford University Press.

Johansson, A. (2018). *We need to reduce our dependence on technology if we want to keep innovating.* Retrieved from https://thenextweb.com/contributors/2018/07/25/we-need-to-reduce-our-dependence-on-technology-if-we-want-to-keep-innovating/

Juergens, J. (2019a). *Naltrexone for alcoholism treatment.* Retrieved from https://www.addictioncenter.com/alcohol/naltrexone-for-alcoholism-treatment/

Juergens, J. (2019b). *Disulfiram for alcoholism treatment.* Retrieved from https://www.addictioncenter.com/alcohol/disulfiram/

Juergens, J. (2019c). *Acamprosate for alcoholism treatment.* Retrieved from https://www.addictioncenter.com/alcohol/acamprosate/

Juergens, J. (2019d). *Understanding cognitive behavioral therapy (CBT).* Retrieved from https://www.addictioncenter.com/treatment/cognitive-behavioral-therapy/

Juergens, J. (2019e). *Alcoholics anonymous.* Retrieved from https://www.addictioncenter.com/treatment/12-step-programs/alcoholics-anonymous/

Juergens, J. (2019f). *Al-Anon.* Retrieved from https://www.addictioncenter.com/treatment/12-step-programs/al-anon/

Juergens, J. (2019g). *Narcotics Anonymous.* Retrieved from https://www.addictioncenter.com/treatment/12-step-programs/narcotics-anonymous/

Kalon, E., Hong, J.Y., Tobin, C., & Schulte, T. (2016). Psychological and neurobiological correlates of food addiction. *International Review of Neurobiology, 129*, 85-110. DOI: 10.1016/bs.im.2016.06.003

Kim, S.W. (1998). Opioid antagonists in the treatment of impulse-control disorders. *Journal of Clinical Psychiatry, 59,* 159-163. DOI: 10.4088/JCP.v59n0403

Klass, P. (2019). *Is 'digital addiction' a real threat to kids?* Retrieved from https://www.nytimes.com/2019/05/20/well/family/is-digital-addiction-a-real-threat-to-kids.html

Klimek, A.M. (2016). Compulsive eating: Causes and risk factors. Retrieved from https://www.eatingdisorderhope.com/blog/compulsive-eating-causes-risk-factors-2

Koob, G. F., Kenneth Lloyd, G., & Mason, B. J. (2009). Development of pharmacotherapies for drug addiction: a Rosetta stone approach. *Nature reviews. Drug discovery, 8*(6), 500–515. doi:10.1038/nrd2828

Kuss, D.J., Griffiths, M.D., Binder, J.F. (2013). Internet addiction in students: Prevalence, and risk factors. *Computers in Human Behavior, 29*(3), 959-966. DOI: 10.1016/j.chb.2012.12.04

Lander, L., Howsare, J. & Bryne, M. (2013). The impact of substance use disorders on families and children: From theory to practice. *Social Work in Public Health, 28*(3-4), 194-205. DOI: 10.1080/19371918.2013.759005

Lee, H.W., Choi, J.S., Shin, Y.C., Lee, J.Y., Jung, H.Y., & Kwon, J.S. (2012). Impulsivity in internet addiction: A comparison with pathological gambling. *Cyberpsychology, Behavior, and Social Networking, 15*(7), 373-377. DOI: 10.1089/cyber.2012.0063

Lejoyeux, M. & Weinstein, A. (2010). Compulsive buying. *The American Journal of Drug and Alcohol Abuse, 36*(5), 248-253. DOI: 10.3109/00952990.2010.4935590

Lembke, A. (2018). *Benzodiazepines: Our other prescription drug epidemic.* Retrieved from https://www.statnews.com/2018/02/22/benzodiazepines-drug-epidemic/

Long, C.G., Blundell, J.E., & Finlayson, G. (2015). A systematic review of the application and correlates of YFAS-diagnosed 'food addiction' in humans: Are eating-related 'addictions' a cause for concern or empty concerns? *Obesity Facts, 8*(6), 386-401. DOI: 10.1159/000442403

Lupi, M., Martinotti, G., Acciavatti, T., Pettoruso, M., Brunetti, M., Santacroce, R., ... & Di Giannantonio, M. (2014). Pharmacological treatments in gambling disorder: A qualitative review. *BioMed Research International,* Article ID 537306. DOI: 10.1155/2014/537306

Maclaren, E. (2018). *What is post-acute withdrawal syndrome?* Retrieved from https://drugabuse.com/drug-withdrawal/post-acute-withdrawal-syndrome/

Manchiraju, S., Sadachar, A., & Ridgway, J.L. (2017). The compulsive online shopping scale (COSS): Development and validation using panel data.

International Journal of Mental Health and Addiction, 15, 209-223. DOI: 10.1007/s11469-016-9662-6

Maraz, A., Griffiths, M.D., & Demetrovics, Z. (2016). The prevalence of compulsive buying: A meta-analysis. *Addiction, 111*(3), 408-419. DOI: 10.1111/add.13223

Martin, T. (2019). *What to know about nicotine use.* Retrieved from https://www.verywellmind.com/nicotine-addiction-101-2825018

Mayo Clinic. (2018). Does society have a sex addiction problem? Retrieved from https://mayoclinichealthsystem.org/hometown-health/speaking-of-health/does-society-have-a-sex-addiction-problem

Mayo Clinic (2019a). Compulsive gambling. Retrieved from https://www.mayoclinic.org/diseases-conditions/compulsive-gambling/symptoms-causes/syc-20355178

Mayo Clinic. (2019b). Binge-eating disorder. Retrieved from https://www.mayoclinic.org/diseases-conditions/binge-eating-disorder/symptoms-causes/syc-20353627

Mayo Clinic. (2020). *Compulsive sexual behaviors.* Retrieved from https://www.mayoclinic.org/diseases-conditions/compulsive-sexual-behavior/symptoms-causes/syc-20360434

McCormick, B. (2019). *Rise of fantasy football played big part in league's growth.* Retrieved from https://www.sportsbusinessdaily.com/Journal/Issues/2019/09/02/Media/Fantasy.aspx

McElroy, S.L., Keck, P.E., Pope, H.G. Smith, J.M., & Strakowski, S.M. (1994). Compulsive buying: A report of 20 cases. *Journal of Clinical Psychiatry, 55,* 242-248.

McLeod, S. (2018). Classical conditioning. Retrieved from https://www.simplypsychology.org/classical-conditioning.html

Merriam-Webster. (2019). *Gamble.* Retrieved from https://www.merriam-webster.com/dictionary/gamble

Meule, A., & Gearhardt, A.N. (2014). Food addiction in the light of DSM-5. *Nutrients, 6*(9), 3653-3671. DOI: 10.3390/nu6093653

Meyers, R. J., Roozen, H. G., & Smith, J. E. (2011). The community reinforcement approach: an update of the evidence. *Alcohol Research & Health: The Journal of the National Institute on Alcohol Abuse and Alcoholism, 33*(4), 380–388. PMID: 23580022

Murphy, R., Straebler, S., Cooper, Z., & Fairburn, C.G. (2010). Cognitive behavioral therapy for eating disorders. *Psychiatric Clinics of North America, 33*(3), 611-627. DOI: 10.1016/j.psc.2010.04.004

Naeem, Z. (2015). Second-hand smoke-ignored implications. *International Journal of Health Sciences, 9*(2), v-vi. Retrieved from https://www.ncbi.nlm.nih.gov/pmc/articles/PMC4538886/

Narcotics Anonymous World Services. (2018). *Information about NA.* Retrieved from https://www.na.org/admin/include/spaw2/uploads/pdf/PR/2302_2018.pdf

National Alliance on Mental Illness. (n.d.). *Eating disorders.* Retrieved from https://www.nami.org/learn-more/mental-health-conditions/eating-disorders

National Cancer Institute. (2018). *Alcohol and cancer risk*. Retrieved from https://www.cancer.gov/about-cancer/causes-prevention/risk/alcohol/alcohol-fact-sheet

National Center for Responsible Gaming. (2012). *Increasing the odds: A series to understanding gambling disorders: Gambling and the brain: Why neuroscience research is vital to gambling research*. Retrieved from https://www.icrg.org/resources/monographs

National Eating Disorders Association. (2018). Risk factors for eating disorders. Retrieved from https://www.nationaleatingdisorders.org/toolkit/parent-toolkit/risk-factors

National Institute on Alcohol Abuse and Alcoholism. (2019a). *Alcohol facts and statistics*. Retrieved from https://www.niaaa.nih.gov/alcohol-facts-and-statistics

National Institute on Alcohol Abuse and Alcoholism. (2019b). *Understanding the dangers of alcohol overdose*. Retrieved from https://www.niaaa.nih.gov/publications/brochures-and-fact-sheets/understanding-dangers-of-alcohol-overdose

National Institute on Drug Abuse. (2014a). *Drugs, brains and behavior: The science of addiction*. Retrieved from https://www.drugabuse.gov/sites/default/files/soa_2014.pdf

National Institute on Drug Abuse. (2014b). *Research report series: Hallucinogens and dissociative drugs*. Retrieved from https://www.drugabuse.gov/sites/default/files/hallucinogensrrs.pdf

National Institute on Drug Abuse. (2015). *Therapeutic communities*. Retrieved from https://d14rmgtrwzf5a.cloudfront.net/sites/default/files/therapueticcomm_rrs_0723.pdf

National Institute on Drug Abuse (2017a). *Inhalants*. Retrieved from https://www.drugabuse.gov/publications/drugfacts/inhalants

National Institute on Drug Abuse (2017b). *MDMA (Ecstasy) abuse*. Retrieved from https://www.drugabuse.gov/node/pdf/1763/mdma-ecstasy-abuse

National Institute on Drug Abuse. (2018a). *Misuse of prescription drugs*. Retrieved from https://www.drugabuse.gov/node/pdf/2609/misuse-of-prescription-drugs

National Institute on Drug Abuse. (2018b). *Five million American adult misusing prescription stimulants*. Retrieved from https://www.drugabuse.gov/news-events/news-releases/2018/04/five-million-american-adults-misusing-prescription-stimulants

National Institute on Drug Abuse. (2018c). *What is cocaine?* Retrieved from https://www.drugabuse.gov/publications/drugfacts/cocaine

National Institute on Drug Abuse. (2018d). *Steroids and other appearance and performance enhancing drugs (APEDs)*. Retrieved from https://www.drugabuse.gov/publications/drugfacts/anabolic-steroids

National Institute on Drug Abuse. (2018e). *Benzodiazepines and opioids*. Retrieved from https://www.drugabuse.gov/drugs-abuse/opioids/benzodiazepines-opioids

National Institute on Drug Abuse. (2018f). *Heroin*. Retrieved from https://www.drugabuse.gov/publications/research-reports/heroin/overview

National Institute on Drug Abuse. (2018g). *Understanding drug use and addiction*. Retrieved from https://www.drugabuse.gov/publications/drugfacts/understanding-drug-use-addiction

National Institute on Drug Abuse. (2018h). *Principles of drug addiction treatment: A research -based guide* (3rd ed.). Retrieved from https://www.drugabuse.gov/node/pdf/675/principles-of-drug-addiction-treatment-a-research-based-guide-third-edition

National Institute on Drug Abuse. (2018i). *Medications to treat opioid use disorder.* Retrieved from https://www.drugabuse.gov/node/pdf/21349/ medications-to-treat-opioid-use-disorder

National Institute on Drug Abuse. (2019a). *Marijuana.* Retrieved from https://www.drugabuse.gov/node/pdf/1380/marijuana

National Institute on Drug Abuse. (2019b). *Opioid overdose crisis.* Retrieved from https://www.drugabuse.gov/drugs-abuse/opioids/opioid-overdose-crisis

National Institute on Drug Abuse. (2019c). *Prescription Opioids.* Retrieved from https://www.drugabuse.gov/publications/drugfacts/prescription-opioids

National Institute on Drug Abuse. (2019d). *Heroin.* Retrieved from https://www.drugabuse.gov/publications/drugfacts/heroin

National Institute on Drug Abuse. (2019e). *Marijuana.* Retrieved from https://www.drugabuse.gov/node/pdf/1380/marijuana

National Institute on Drug Abuse. (2019f). *Hallucinogens.* Retrieved from https://www.drugabuse.gov/publications/drugfacts/hallucinogens

National Institute on Drug Abuse. (2019g). *Treatment approaches for drug addiction.* Retrieved from https://www.drugabuse.gov/publications/drugfacts/treatment-approaches-drug-addiction

National Institute on Drug Abuse. (2020). *Tobacco, nicotine and E-cigarettes.* Retrieved from https://www.drugabuse.gov/node/pdf/1344/tobacco-nicotine-and-e-cigarettes

National Institute on Drug Abuse for Teens. (2019). *Inhalants.* Retrieved from https://teens.drugabuse.gov/drug-facts/inhalants

National Institute on Drug Abuse for Teens. (2020a). *Tobacco, nicotine, & vaping (E-cigarettes).* Retrieved from https://teens.drugabuse.gov/drug-facts/tobacco-nicotine-e-cigarettes

National Institute on Drug Abuse for Teens. (2020b). *Cocaine.* Retrieved from https://teens.drugabuse.gov/drug-facts/cocaine

National Institute on Drug Abuse for Teens. (2020c). *Steroids, Anabolic.* Retrieved from https://teens.drugabuse.gov/drug-facts/steroids-anabolic

National Institute on Drug Abuse for Teens. (2019a). *Prescription depressant medications.* Retrieved from https://teens.drugabuse.gov/drug-facts/prescription-depressant-medications

National Institute on Drug Abuse for Teens. (2019b). *Marijuana. Retrieved from* https://teens.drugabuse.gov/drug-facts/marijuana

National Institute on Drug Abuse for Teens. (2019c). *Prescription stimulant medications (Amphetamines).* Retrieved from https://teens.drugabuse.gov/drug-facts/prescription-stimulant-medications-amphetamines

National Institutes of Health. (2016). Prescription medications to treat overweight and obesity. Retrieved from https://www.niddk.nih.gov/health-information/weight-management/prescription-medications-treat-overweight-obesity

National Institutes of Health: National Institute on Alcohol Abuse and Alcoholism. (2019a). *College drinking.* Retrieved from https://www.niaaa.nih.gov/publications/brochures-and-fact-sheets/college-drinking

National Institutes of Health: National Institute on Alcohol Abuse and Alcoholism. (2019b). *Understanding the dangers of alcohol overdose.* Retrieved from https://www.niaaa.nih.gov/publications/brochures-and-fact-sheets/understanding-dangers-of-alcohol-overdose

National Institutes of Health: National Institute on Alcohol Abuse and Alcoholism. (n.d.a). *Alcohol's effects on the body.* Retrieved from https://www.niaaa.nih.gov/alcohols-effects-body

National Institutes of Health: National Institute on Alcohol Abuse and Alcoholism. (n.d.b). *Overview of alcoholism.* Retrieved from https://www.niaaa.nih.gov/overview-alcohol-consumption

National Institute on Alcohol Abuse and Alcoholism. (n.d.c). *Alcohol use disorder.* Retrieved from https://www.niaaa.nih.gov/alcohol-health/overview-alcohol-consumption/ alcohol-use-disorders

North American Foundation for Gambling Addiction. (2017). *Statistics of gambling addiction, 2016.* Retrieved from http://nafgah.org/statistics-gambling-addiction-2016/

Northpoint Recovery. (June 4, 2017). *The many types of substance and behavioral addictions.* Retrieved from https://www.northpointrecovery.com/blog/many-types-of-substance-and-behavioral-addictions/

Nower, L., Caler, K.R., Pickering, D., & Blaszczynski, A. (2018). Daily fantasy sports players: Gambling, addiction, and mental health problems. *Journal of Gambling Studies, 34,* 727-737. DOI: 10.1007/s10899-018-9744-4

Ogundele, M.O. (2018). Behavioural and emotional disorders in childhood: A brief overview for paediatricians. *World Journal of Clinical Pediatrics, 7*(1), 9-26. DOI: 10.5409/wjcp.v7.i1.9

Okhifun, G. (2019). *The social effects of alcoholism-Consequences and issues.* Retrieved from https://alcorehab.org/the-effects-of-alcohol/social/

Okuda, M., Balán, I., Petry, N.M., Oquendo, M., & Bianco, C. (2009). Cognitive behavioral therapy for pathological gambling: Cultural considerations. *American Journal of Psychiatry, 166*(12), 1325-1330. DOI: 10.1176/appi.ajp.2009.08081235

Ortiz-Ospina, E. (2019). *The rise of social media.* Retrieved from https://ourworldindata.org/rise-of-social-media

Ostovar, S., Allahyar, N., Aminpoor, H., Moafian, F., Nor, M.B.M., & Griffiths, M.D. (2016). Internet addiction and its psychosocial risks (depression, anxiety, stress, and loneliness) among Iranian adolescents and young adults: A structural equation model in a cross-sectional study. *International Journal of Mental Health and Addiction, 14*(3), 257-267. DOI: 10.1007/s11469-0159628-0

Patterson, E. (2017). *Contingency management.* Retrieved from https://drugabuse.com/contingency-management/

Patterson, E. (2018a). *Heroin abuse.* Retrieved from https://drugabuse.com/heroin/

Patterson, E. (2018b). *Family therapy: A vital part of addiction treatment.* Retrieved from https://drugabuse.com/treatment-therapy/family-therapy/

Patterson, E. (2018c). *Motivational Interviewing.* Retrieved from https://drug abuse.com/treatment-therapy/motivational-interviewing/

Patterson, E. (2018d). *The matrix model.* Retrieved from https://drugabuse.com/treatment/matrix-model/

Phillips, B., Hajela, R., & Hilton, Jr. D.L. (2015). Sex addiction as a disease: Evidence for assessment, diagnosis, and response to critics. *Sexual Addiction and Compulsivity, 22*(2), 167-192. DOI: 10.1080/10720162.2015.1036184

Pidd, H. (2017). Gambling in an industry that feasts on the poor and vulnerable. Retrieved from https://www.theguardian.com/commentisfree/2017/sep/05/gambling-industry-feasts-on-poor-vulnerable-helen-pidd

Poli, R. (2017). Internet addiction update: Diagnostic criteria, assessment and prevalence. *Neuropsychiatry (London), 7*(1), 4-8. DOI: 10.4172/neuropsychiatry.1000171

Popely, R. (2016). *Which 2017 cars offer in-car wi-fi?* Retrieved from https://www.cars.com/articles/which-2017-cars-offer-in-car-wi-fi-1420692490461/

Preiato, D. (2019). *Are steroids bad for you? Uses, side effects, and dangers.* Retrieved from https://www.healthline.com/nutrition/are-steroids-bad

Psychology Today. (2019a). *Nicotine.* Retrieved from https://www.Psychology today.com/us/conditions/nicotine

Psychology Today. (2019b). *Opioids.* Retrieved from https://www.Psychology today.com/us/conditions/opioids

Psychology Today. (n.d.). *Hypersexuality (Sex addiction).* Retrieved from https://www.psychologytoday.com/us/conditions/hypersexuality-sex-addiction

Pursey, K.M., Stanwell, P., Gearhardt, A.N., Collins, C.E., & Burrows, T.L. (2014). The prevalence of food addiction as assessed by the Yale Food Addiction Scale: A systematic review. *Nutrients, 6*(10), 4552-4590. DOI: 10.3390/nu6104552

Rahman, A. & Paul. M. (2019). *Delirium tremens (DT).* Retrieved from www.ncbi.nlm.gov/books/NBK482134

Responsible Drinking. (n.d.). *What are you drinking?* Retrieved from http://www.responsibledrinking.org/what-are-you-drinking/what-is-an-alcohol-beverage/

Reuters. (2012). *One in 10 U.S. kids have alcoholic parent: Study.* Retrieved from https://www.reuters.com/article/us-usa-drinking-study/one-in-10-u-s-kids-have-alcoholic-parent-study-idUSTRE81F0CB20120216

Rigotti, N.A. (2020). *Pharmacotherapy for smoking cessation in adults.* Retrieved from https://www.uptodate.com/contents/pharmacotherapy-for-smoking-cessation-in-adults#H13314646

Roberts, J.A., & Roberts, C.A. (2015). Does thin always sell? The moderating role of thin ideal internalization on advertising effectiveness. *Atlantic Marketing Journal, 4*(1), 1-24. Retrieved from https://digitalcommons.kennesaw.edu/cgi/viewcontent.cgi?article=1145&context=amj

Romanczuk-Seiferth, N., Koehler, S., Dreesen, C., Wüstenberg, T., & Heinz, A. (2014). Pathological gambling and alcohol dependence: Neural disturbances in reward and loss avoidance processing. *Addiction Biology, 20,* 557-569. DOI: 10.1111/adb.12144

Rosenberg, K.P., Carnes, P., & O'Connor, S. (2014). Evaluation and treatment of sex addiction. *Journal of Sex and Marital Therapy, 40*(2), 77-91. DOI: 10.1080/0092623X.2012.701268

Ross, E.J., Graham, D.L., Money, K.M. & Stanwood, G.D. (2015). Developmental consequences of fetal exposure to drugs: What we know and what we still must learn. *Neuropsychopharmacology, 40*(1), 61-87. DOI: 10.1038/npp.2014. 147

SA. (n.d.). *Spenders Anonymous – Abstinence in spending.* Retrieved from http://www.spenders.org/abstinence.html

SAA. (2020). *Our program.* Retrieved from https://saa-recovery.org/our-program/

Saleh, K. (2018). Global online retail spending – statistics and trends. Retrieved from https://www.invespcro.com/blog/global-online-retail-spending-statistics- and-trends/

Saliceti, F. (2015). Internet addiction disorder (IAD). *Procedia-Social and Behavorial Sciences, 191,* 1372-1376. DOI: 10.1016/j.sbspro.2015.04.292

Schiller E.Y. & Mechanic, O.J. (2019). *Opioid Overdose.* Retrieved from https://www.ncbi.nlm.nih.gov/books/NBK470415/

Scholl L., Seth P., Kariisa, M. Wilson, N., & Baldwin, G. (2019). Drug and opioid-involved overdose deaths – United States, 2013-2017. *MMWR Morbidity Weekly Report 2019, 67,* 1419-1427. DOI: 10.15585/mmwr.mm675152e1

Schwetz, T.A., Calder, T., Rosenthal, E., Kattakuzhy, S. & Fauci, A.S. (2019). Opioids and infectious diseases: A converging public health crisis. *Journal of Infectious Diseases, 220*(1), 346-349. Https://doi.org//10.1093/infdis/jiz133

Smith, R.L. (2015). *Treatment strategies for substance and process addictions.* American Counseling Association. Retrieved from https://www.counseling. org/Publications/Reviews/78109-REVIEWS.PDF

Smith, D.P., Battersby, M.W., Pols, R.G., Harvey, P.W., Oakes, J.E., Baigent, M.F. (2015). Predictors of relapse in problem gambling: A prospective cohort study. *Journal of Gambling Studies, 31,* 299-313. DOI: 10.1007/s10899-013-9408-3

Sohn, S-H., & Choi, Y-J. (2014). Phases of shopping addiction evidenced by experiences of compulsive buyers. *International Journal of Mental Health and Addiction, 12,* 243-254. DOI: 10.1007/s11469-013-9449-y

Solis, J.M., Shadur, J.M., Burns, A.R. & Hussong, A.M. (2012). Understanding the diverse needs of children whose parents abuse substances. *Current Drug Abuse Review, 5*(2), 135-147. DOI: 10.2174/1874473711205020135

Squeglia, L.M., Jacobus, J. & Tapert, S.F. (2009). The influence of substance use on adolescent brain development. *Clinical EEG and Neuroscience, 40*(1), 31-38. DOI: 10.1177/155005940904000110

Statista. (2019). Number of establishments in the United States fast food industry from 2004-2018. Retrieved from https://www.statista.com/statistics/196619/total-number-of-fast-food-restaurants-in-the-us-since-2002/

Substance Abuse and Mental Health Services Administration. (2019). *Key substance use and mental health indicators in the United States: Results from the 2018 National Survey on Drug Use and Health (HHS Publication No. PEP19-5068, NSDUH Series H-54).* Retrieved from https://www.samhsa. gov/data/sites/default/files/cbhsq-reports/NSDUH NationalFindingsReport2018/NSDUHNationalFindingsReport2018.pdf

Suissa, A.J. (2011). Vulnerability and gambling addiction: Psychosocial benchmarks and avenues for intervention. *International Journal of Mental Health and Addiction, 9,* 12-23. DOI: 10.1007/s11469-009-9248-7

Sussman. S., Leventhal, A., Bluthenthal, R.N., Freimuth, M., Forster, M. & Ames, S.L. (2011). A framework for the specificity of addictions. *International Journal of Environmental Research and Public Health, 8*(8), 3399-3415. DOI: 10.3390/ijerph8083399

Tackett, B. (2019). *What is Molly? 5 things you didn't know about MDMA.* Retrieved from https://drugabuse.com/molly-mdma/

Tas, B. & Oztosun, A. (2018). Predictability of internet addiction with adolescent perception of social support and ostracism experiences. *Turkish Online Journal of Educational Technology, 17*(4), 32-41.

Tas, I. (2017). Relationship between internet addiction, gaming addiction, and school engagement among adolescents. *Universal Journal of Educational Research, 5*(12), 2304-2311. DOI: 10.13189/ujer.2017.051221

Tas, I. (2019). Association between depression, anxiety, stress, social support, resilience and internet addiction: A structural equation modeling. *Malaysian Online Journal of Educational Technology, 7*(3), 1-10. DOI: 10.17220/mojet.2019.03.001

The Oaks. (2018). Causes for compulsive shopping. Retrieved from https://theoakstreatment.com/blog/causes-for-compulsive-shopping/

Thomas, S. (2019). *Overdose symptoms: Understanding the risk of drug overdose.* Retrieved from https://americanaddictioncenters.org/overdose

Trotzke, P., Starcke, K., Muller, A., Brand, M. (2015). Pathological buying online as a specific form of internet addiction: A model-based experimental investigation. *PLoS One, 10*(10), e-article. DOI: 10.1371/journal.pone.0140296

Tyler, M. (2016). Shopping addiction. Retrieved from https://www.healthline.com/health/addiction/shopping

Ungar, L. (2019). *Not yesterday's cocaine: Death toll rising from tainted drug.* Retrieved from https://khn.org/news/not-yesterdays-cocaine-death-toll-rising-from-tainted-drug/

United States Department of Transportation (n.d.). Distracted driving. Retrieved from https://www.nhtsa.gov/risky-driving/distracted-driving

University of Kansas. (2019). *Data-driven definition of unhealthy yet pervasive 'hyper-palatable' foods.* Retrieved from https://www.sciencedaily.com/releases/2019/11/191105104436.htm

U.S. Department of Health and Human Services. (2018). *The National Institute on Drug Abuse media guide: How to find what you need to know about drug use and addiction.* Retrieved from https://d14rmgtrwzf5a.cloudfront.net/sites/default/files/media_guide.pdf

Van Holst, R.J., van Holstein, M., van der Brink, W., Veltman, D.J. & Goudriaan, A.E. (2012). Response inhibition during cue reactivity in problem gamblers: An fMRI study. *PLOS One, 7*(3), e30909. DOI: 10.1371/journal.pone.0030909.

Vogel, B., Trotzke, P., Steins-Loeber, S., Schafer, G., Stenger, J., de Zwaan, M., ... & Muller, A. (2019). An experimental examination of cognitive processes and response inhibition in patients seeking treatment for buying-shopping disorder. *PLoS One, 14*(3), e-article. DOI: 10.1371/journal/pone.0212415

Weinstein, A., Zlatkes, M., Gingis, A., & Lejoyeux, M. (2015). The effects of a 12-step self-health group for compulsive eating on measures of food addiction, anxiety, depression, and self-efficacy. *Journal of Groups in Addiction and Recovery, 10*(2), 190-200. DOI: 10.1080/1556035X.2015.1034825

Weiss, D. (2019). Sex addiction: What is it? Retrieved from https://sexaddict.com

Weiss, H.D., & Marsh, L. (2012). Impulse control disorders and compulsive behaviors associated with dopaminergic therapies in Parkinson disease. *Neurology Clinical Practice, 2*(4), 267-274. DOI: 10.1212/CPJ.0b013e318278be9b

Weller, C. (2017). *Japan is facing a 'death by overwork' problem – here's what it's all about.* Retrieved from https://www.businessinsider.com/what-is-karoshi-japanese-word-for-death-by-overwork-2017-10

Wilson, P. (2016). *15 things you didn't know about gambling (but should).* Retrieved from https://www.gamblingsites.com/blog/15-things-you-didnt-know-about-online-gambling-11655/

Woehler, E.S., Giordano, A.L., & Hagedom, W.B. (2018). Moments of relational depth in sex addiction treatment. *Sexual Addiction and Compulsivity, 25*(1), 1-17. DOI: 10.1080/10720162.2018.1476943

World Health Organization. (1977). *The international classification of diseases, 9th revision.* Retrieved from https://www.cdc.gov/nchs/icd/icd9cm.htm

Wu, C-Y., Lee, M-B., Liao, S-C., & Chang, L-R. (2015). Risk factors of internet addiction among internet users: An online questionnaire survey. *PLoS One, 10*(10). DOI: 10.1371/journal.pone.0137506

Yang, F., Liu, A., Li, Y., Lai, Y., Wang, G., Sun, C., ... & Teng, W. (2017). Food addiction in patients with newly diagnosed type 2 diabetes in northeast China. *Frontiers in Endocrinology, 8.* DOI: 10.3389.fendo.2017.00218

Younes, F., Halawi, G., Jabbour, H., El Osta, N., Karam, L., Hajj, A., & Khabbaz, L.R. (2016). Internet addiction and relationships with insomnia, anxiety, depression, stress, and self-esteem in university students: A cross-sectional designed study. *PLoS One, 11*(9). DOI: 10.1371/journal.pone.0161126

Young, K.S. (1998). Internet addiction: The emergence of a new clinical disorder. *CyberPsychology and Behavior, 1*(3), 237-244. DOI: 10.1089/cpb.1998.1.237

Young, N.D., Mumby, M.A., & Smolinski, J.A. (2019). *Maximizing mental health services: Proven practices that promote emotional well-being.* Wilmington, DE: Vernon Press

Zajac, K., Ginley, M.K., Chang, R., & Petry, N.M. (2017). Treatments for internet gaming disorder and internet addiction: A systematic review. *Psychology of Addictive Behaviors, 31*(8), 979-994. DOI: 10.1037/adb0000315

Zakhari, S. (2006). *Overview: How is alcohol metabolized by the body?* Retrieved from https://pubs.niaaa.nih.gov/publications/arh294/245-255.pdf

About the Authors

Nicholas D. Young, PhD, EdD

Dr. Nicholas D. Young has worked in diverse educational roles for more than 30 years, serving as a teacher, counselor, principal, special education director, graduate professor, graduate program director, graduate dean, and longtime psychologist and superintendent of schools. He was named the Massachusetts Superintendent of the Year; and he completed a distinguished Fulbright program focused on the Japanese educational system through the collegiate level. Dr. Young is the recipient of numerous other honors and recognitions including the General Douglas MacArthur Award for distinguished civilian and military leadership and the Vice Admiral John T. Hayward Award for exemplary scholarship. He holds several graduate degrees including a PhD in educational administration and an EdD in psychology.

Dr. Young has served in the U.S. Army and U.S. Army Reserves combined for over 35 years; and he graduated with distinction from the U.S. Air War College, the U.S. Army War College, and the U.S. Navy War College. After completing a series of senior leadership assignments in the U.S. Army Reserves as the commanding officer of the 287th Medical Company (DS), the 405th Area Support Company (DS), the 405th Combat Support Hospital, and the 399th Combat Support Hospital, he transitioned to his current military position as a faculty instructor at the U.S. Army War College in Carlisle, PA. He currently holds the rank of Colonel.

Dr. Young is also a regular presenter at state, national, and international conferences; and he has written many books, book chapters, and/or articles on various topics in education, counseling, and psychology. Some of his most recent books include *Maximizing Mental Health Services: Proven Practices that Promote Emotional Well-Being* (2020); *Masculinity in the Making: Managing the Transition to Manhood* (2020); *The Burden of Being a Boy: Bolstering Educational and Emotional Well-Being in Young Males* (2019); *The Special Education Toolbox: Supporting Exceptional Teachers, Students, and Families* (2019); *Sounding the Alarm in the Schoolhouse: Safety, Security and Student Well-Being (2019); Creating Compassionate Classrooms: Understanding the Continuum of Disabilities and Effective Educational Interventions* (2019); *Acceptance, Understanding, and the Moral Imperative of Promoting Social Justice Education in the Schoolhouse* (2019); *Empathic Teaching: Promoting Social Justice in the Contemporary Classroom* (2019); *Educating the Experienced: Challenges and Best Practices in Adult Learning* (2019); *Securing the Schoolyard: Protocols that Promote Safety and Positive Student Behaviors* (2018); *The Soul of the Schoolhouse: Cultivating Student Engagement* (2018); *Embracing and Educating the Autistic Child: Valuing Those Who Color Outside the Lines* (2018); *From Cradle to Classroom: A Guide to Special Education for Young Children* (2018); *Captivating Classrooms: Educational Strategies to Enhance Student Engagement* (2018); *Potency of the Principalship: Action-Oriented Leadership at the Heart of School Improvement* (2018); *Soothing the Soul: Pursuing a Life of Abundance Through a Practice of Gratitude* (2018); *Dog Tags to Diploma: Understanding and Addressing the Educational Needs of Veterans, Servicemembers, and their Families* (2018); *Turbulent Times: Confronting Challenges in Emerging Adulthood* (2018); *Guardians of the Next Generation: Igniting the Passion for Quality Teaching* (2018); *Achieving Results: Maximizing Success in the Schoolhouse* (2018); *From Head to Heart: High Quality Teaching Practices in the Spotlight* (2018); *Stars in the Schoolhouse: Teaching Practices and Approaches that Make a Difference* (2018); *Making the Grade: Promoting Positive Outcomes for Students with Learning Disabilities* (2018); *Paving the Pathway for Educational Success: Effective Classroom Interventions for Students with Learning Disabilities* (2018); *Wrestling with Writing: Effective Strategies for Struggling Students* (2018); *Floundering to Fluent: Reaching and Teaching the Struggling Student* (2018); *Emotions and Education: Promoting Positive Mental Health in Students with Learning* (2018); *From Lecture Hall to Laptop: Opportunities, Challenges, and the Continuing Evolution of Virtual Learning in Higher Education* (2017); *The Power of the Professoriate: Demands, Challenges, and Opportunities in 21st Century Higher Education* (2017); *To Campus with Confidence: Supporting a Successful Transition to College for Students with Learning Disabilities* (2017); *Educational Entrepreneurship: Promoting Public-Private Partnerships for the 21st Century* (2015); *Beyond the Bedtime Story: Promoting Reading Development during the Middle School Years* (2015); *Betwixt and Between: Understanding and Meeting the Social and Emotional Developmental Needs of Students During the Middle School Transition Years* (2014); *Learning Style Perspectives: Impact Upon the Classroom* (3rd ed., 2014); and *Collapsing Educational Boundaries from Preschool to PhD: Building Bridges Across the Educational Spectrum* (2013); *Transforming Special Education Practices: A Primer for School Administrators and Policy Makers* (2012); and *Powerful Partners in Student Success: Schools, Families and Communities* (2012). He also co-authored several children's books to include the popular series *I am Full of Possibilities*. Dr. Young may be contacted directly at nyoung1191@aol.com.

Melissa A. Mumby, EdD

Dr. Mumby has worked in various levels of K-12 education for over a decade. She began her career as a high school English and drama teacher, and then transitioned into a role as a special educator, working with both middle and high school students. From there she became a special education coordinator for grades K-5, and eventually the special education director for grades K-12 at a local charter school. She is currently an educational team leader in an urban public school district in Massachusetts. Dr. Mumby holds an undergraduate degree in English Literature from the University of Massachusetts, Amherst, as well as an MEd and EdD. from American International College, both in education. Her dissertation, "Is there an app for that? Teachers' perceptions of the impact of digital tools on literacy in the secondary classroom" focused on the ways in which technology can increase learning outcomes for struggling learners. She has written book chapters on strategies for helping underperforming students find success in the classroom and she is a primary author on *Maximizing Mental Health Services: Proven Practices that Promote Emotional Well-Being* (2020); *The Special Education Toolbox: Supporting Exceptional Teachers, Students, and Families* (2019); *Educating the Experienced: Challenges and Best Practices in Adult Learning* (2019); *Embracing and Educating the Autistic Child: Valuing Those Who Color Outside the Lines* (2018). Dr. Mumby can be reached at mumbym@springfieldpublicschools.com.

Jennifer A. Smolinski, JD

Attorney Jennifer Smolinski has worked in education for more than three years. Her role within higher education includes the creation of, and coordinator for, the Center for Accessibility Services and Academic Accommodations at American International College located in Springfield, Massachusetts. She has also taught criminal justice and legal research and writing classes within the field of higher education. Prior to her work at the collegiate level, Attorney Smolinski worked as a solo-practitioner conducting education and disability advocacy.

Attorney Smolinski received a Bachelor of Arts in Anthropology and Bachelor of Arts in Sociology from the University of Connecticut, a master's in psychology and Counseling as well as a master's of Higher Education Student Affairs from Salem State University and her law degree from Massachusetts School of Law. She is currently an EdD in Educational Leadership and Supervision candidate at American International College, where she is focusing her research on special education and laws to protect students with disabilities in the classroom.

Attorney Smolinski has become a regular presenter educating the faculty, staff and students at institutes of higher education on disabilities and accommodations at the collegiate level and has presented to local high school special education departments on the transition to college under the Americans with Disabilities Act. She has co-authored *Maximizing Mental Health Services: Proven Practices that Promote Emotional Well-Being* (2020); *Securing the Schoolyard: Protocols that Promote Safety and Positive Student Behaviors* (2018); *Sounding the Alarm in the Schoolhouse: Safety, Security and Student Well-Being* (2018); *Captivating Classrooms: Educational Strategies to Enhance Student Engagement* (2018); *Guardian of the Next Generation: Igniting the Passion for Quality Teaching* (2018); and *Making the Grade: Promoting Positive Outcomes for Students with Learning Disabilities* (2018). She can be reached at Jennifer.Smolinski@aic.edu.